"In 1989, Gretchen Carlson was chosen to be Miss America—I was one of the judges who picked her! Since then, I have watched Gretchen grow as a journalist and as a woman, proving that beautiful women can be smart and that working women can be good moms. In *Getting Real,* Gretchen writes frankly and with humor about the challenges she's met along the way. We can't all be Miss America but we can all learn from Gretchen how to confront whatever comes our way and come out winners."

> —Deborah Norville, anchor of *Inside Edition* and
> author of *Thank You Power*

"Gretchen's *Getting Real* is a powerful tool for young women who desire to become everything God designed them to be. Poignantly and humbly, she shares her struggles on the long road to success. And she honors the God of all creation in the process. Brava!"

> —Kathie Lee Gifford, cohost of *Today* and
> author of *Just When I Thought I'd Dropped My Last Egg*

"Gretchen Carlson is a gifted news anchor who always gets the story right and who continues to make Minnesotans proud. In *Getting Real,* Gretchen takes us inside the competitive worlds of music, Miss America, and television news and shows us that with hard work—and resilience—dreams do come true."

> —Fran Tarkenton, pro football Hall of Fame quarterback and
> founder of Tarkenton Companies

"Finding success in life comes after some failures and a lot of hard work. Watching Gretchen succeed inspires me and will inspire all women: she seized the day, made the most of her talents, and never, ever gave up."

> —Vanessa Williams, singer, actress, and *New York Times*
> bestselling author

"My spirit resonates with Gretchen Carlson's single-eyed focus, steely determination, and all-out commitment to achieve her goals. Her standards of excellence and sacrificial discipline are exemplary. *Getting Real* has caused me to examine my own life in order to eliminate any casualness or carelessness as I seek to follow and serve Jesus Christ."

> —Anne Graham Lotz, founder of AnGeL Ministries and
> author of *Wounded by God's People*

"Gretchen has such an amazing message, one that will inspire young women. One of courage, determination, faith, and guts. We all have a journey, and Gretchen has graciously given us her map to help others find theirs."

> —Kristin Chenoweth, Emmy and Tony award-winning
> actress and singer

"Winston Churchill famously opined that success consists of going from failure to failure without a loss of enthusiasm. Gretchen Carlson embodies the very nature of success by remaining steadfast to the vision that inspires her and to the God-breathed purpose that allows those dreams to take flight and that affirms her true calling in times of failure. She is truly living her best life."

> —Bishop T. D. Jakes, CEO of TDJ Enterprises and
> *New York Times* bestselling author

"Gretchen Carlson's story is so inspiring. She is indeed what she aspires to be: an authentic role model for all women and girls. Not because of her musical talent, her Miss America crown, or her Fox News celebrity, but because she shares her failures and vulnerabilities as well as her successes, and, of course, her unwavering faith."

> —Marilyn Carlson Nelson, former chairman and
> CEO of Carlson and current co-CEO of Carlson Holdings

"As a fellow Minnesotan, I've followed Gretchen's career since her reigns as Miss Minnesota and Miss America. She inspired us all then and continues to impress us with her many accomplishments. It doesn't get any more *real* than Gretchen's remarkable memoir."

—Harvey B. Mackay, author of the #1 *New York Times* bestseller *Swim with the Sharks*

"My Fox News colleague Gretchen Carlson has written a book and here's what I like about it: *clarity!* Gretchen tells her story in a way that can help other people who are trying to do the right thing in life. Nice job!"

—Bill O'Reilly, host of *The O'Reilly Factor* and *New York Times* bestselling author

"I first met Gretchen Carlson when we were teenagers competing against each other in violin competitions, and over the years I've watched with admiration as she has applied the skills and determination that made her a music prodigy to help her achieve success in pretty much everything she has aspired to do. From virtuoso to Miss America to television star . . . what a fascinating life!"

—Joshua Bell, Grammy Award-winning violinist and conductor

Getting Real

GRETCHEN CARLSON

Getting Real

VIKING

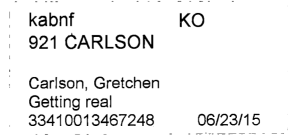

VIKING

Published by the Penguin Publishing Group
Penguin Random House LLC
375 Hudson Street
New York, New York 10014

USA | Canada | UK | Ireland | Australia |
New Zealand | India | South Africa | China
penguin.com
A Penguin Random House Company

First published by Viking Penguin, an imprint of Penguin Publishing Group,
a division of Penguin Random House LLC, 2015

Photographs courtesy of the author unless otherwise indicated.

ISBN 978-0-525-42745-2

Printed in the United States of America
3   5   7   9   10   8   6   4   2

Set in Sabon LT Std
Designed by Amy Hill

Penguin is committed to publishing works of quality and integrity. In that spirit,
we are proud to offer this book to our readers; however, the story,
the experiences, and the words are the author's alone.

To my parents,
Lee and Karen Carlson,
who gave me the foundation in life
to go for my dreams
and the love and support to achieve them.
I am forever grateful.

Contents

PROLOGUE

Speaking My Mind

"Have you had sex yet . . . or are you waiting for marriage?"

The New York press is a tough crowd, especially for a twenty-two-year-old suddenly thrust into the spotlight. But two days after being crowned Miss America, at my first national press conference, the last thing I expected was confrontation, especially from one dogged reporter named Penny Crone, who seemed eager to take me down.

Her question elicited a chorus of boos from the other reporters in the room. They'd had enough. Before she "went there," Penny had barraged me with a series of test questions, supposedly designed to prove I didn't have a brain, because all the media were reporting that I was a senior at Stanford, positioning me as the "smart Miss America." As if to say, "Okay, let's see how smart you really are," she gave me a quiz right in the middle of the press conference: "Do you know who Mary Jo Kopechne is . . . Do you know who Daniel Berrigan is . . . Do you know whose face is on the twenty-dollar bill . . . ?"

I held up under the pressure, but I felt humiliated. What young woman wouldn't? The memory of that press conference stayed with me, and when I later looked back with more perspective, those questions made me angry. Why would a seasoned reporter think it was newsworthy to take down a young woman in such a gleeful manner? Ratings? Meanness? It made a deep impression on me.

At the time I just smiled and moved on. Then, more than a decade later, in 2000, when I was a correspondent for CBS News, I was at a pep rally for the Mets and Yankees in Bryant Park. They were playing a Subway Series that year. I was standing on a platform with others from the press, and there was Penny Crone. I recognized her. And it struck me right then: I was going to say something to her. When we were done, I walked over and said, "Penny, I'd like to reintroduce myself. I'm Gretchen Carlson." I could tell she had no idea who I was. I said, "I'm the Miss America you demoralized in 1989—and I'd just like to let you know that I still made it. I'm a CBS News correspondent . . . and you're not." It was out of character for me to seek revenge, but I went for it. Although I'd often thought about giving her a taste of her own medicine, rarely in life do we get those opportunities. I did it for myself and for all the other women who've been made fun of, called names, put down—just because.

I didn't wait for a response. I didn't want one. I walked away smiling. It felt great!

There's something about the title of Miss America that brings out the snark. When you're wearing the crown, some people see it as an opportunity to knock you down a peg. On my first morning in Atlantic City, I was intent on inspiring girls who were overweight, letting them know they could still pursue their dreams and win. So I told the story of being a chubby child and how my brothers used to tease me, calling me Hindenburg and Blimpo. The next day, walking through the airport, my first brush with fame was glimpsing a banner headline on that week's *Star* magazine: "Blimpo Becomes Miss America." It was a rude awakening.

William Goldman, an accomplished and famous screenwriter, whose credits include *Butch Cassidy and the Sundance Kid* and *The Princess Bride,* was a judge at the pageant my year, and he actually wrote a book about it, which was published in 1990. It's a good thing I didn't know about the book until later, because it might have shaken my confidence a little to read page after page about my inadequacies, wrapped around the title he gave me, "Miss Piggy." He also called me a "God-clutcher" because I said my faith was important to me. To Goldman I was too "chunky" (at 108 pounds!) to even make it to the top ten. He seemed downright offended that talent should count as half the score, and he didn't much care for my winning violin performance of *Gypsy Airs,* which he referred to as "fiddling." He admitted to favoring Miss Colorado. Still, his criticism of me throughout the book was a little over the top. His objectification of me and the other women in the pageant was demeaning. Rereading it recently, I was surprised to find that it still stung. I was embarrassed, even ashamed. It made me realize that shaming is a potent force. For decades I hid my feelings about Goldman's takedown because it was so belittling. But I certainly have no reason to feel that way. Now I understand that this kind of degrading talk is what keeps young women from being fully themselves—or even trying.

When moms ask me what their little girls should do to become Miss America, I tell them they should take piano lessons, play sports, and study hard. In other words, be the best they can be. You have to build from the inside out, have an inner core, and know who you are to have the confidence to achieve your dreams.

My parents taught me that I could be anything I wanted to be, and that's how I've lived my life. Thanks to their love and the values I learned in my small midwestern hometown of Anoka, Minnesota, I grew up with a fierce determination to make my own destiny. For me being Miss America had less to do with how I looked and more to do with who I was and how I could use my talent and hard work to advance myself. I started the process of becoming myself not on a pageant stage wearing a gown, but as a very young girl who discovered the gift of music.

The first time I picked up a violin it just clicked. By the age of ten I was playing with world-renowned concert violinist Isaac Stern before large audiences. I wasn't nervous because nobody ever told me I was *supposed* to be nervous. There was affirmation in the applause. Even when I was a very young girl, I played in church, and people clapped. That was a shock—you weren't supposed to clap in church! But I smiled, enjoying the moment.

I loved performing and I was passionate about music, but the accomplishment came with a *lot* of practice. I practiced my violin three to four hours a day. I missed playing with friends and being a Girl Scout and having lazy days when I did nothing at all. I've never regretted that time, though sometimes I struggled, and it was lonely. The point is, by the time I was twenty-two, I had earned a place on the public stage. I would never have been Miss America—much less Miss Minnesota—were it not for my violin.

Nevertheless, after I won Miss America, people felt comfortable referring to me as a blonde bimbo. I always get asked whether being Miss America was good for my career. Overall, I have to say yes, but sometimes it took people a little time to get there. The first job I applied for in TV after I graduated from Stanford was in Richmond, Virginia. When I called the news director and introduced myself, he remembered me from the pageant. "Weren't you Miss America?" he asked doubtfully. "My wife doesn't even let me *watch* the Miss America pageant. I'm sure I'm not going to like your work." I kept my cool—by then I'd had a lot of practice. "Why don't I send you a tape and maybe you'll change your mind," I suggested. Fortunately, he hired me.

Even now I have critics who refer to me as an empty St. John suit in five-inch stiletto heels, despite the fact that I've been practicing journalism for twenty-five years. They assume that because I do a show on Fox News I must be required to toe a party line, and they're shocked when I tell them I'm a registered independent, free to say what I want.

I have always been one to speak my mind, and I don't sit still for being stereotyped. A friend who knows me really well called me "Badass" one day, a nickname that stuck. It was all in good fun, but Barbara Walters pounced on it the day I cohosted *The View.* I think she was mystified that anyone would call me that, but to me it was a badge of honor because that's who I am. I stand up for myself and speak freely, whether the subject is faith or freedom or my own potential. People like to criticize the "bimbo" or mock people who openly profess their faith. If someone wants to label me as a God-clutcher or a culture warrior, go for it.

I don't mind being called a culture warrior, and that includes being a warrior for women's equality. The National Organization for Women has never invited me to play on their team, and that's okay with me. I don't like boxes or labels. But no one feels as strongly as I do about equality for women.

When I was on *Fox & Friends* I got a lot of publicity on one occasion when I stood up for women. I did it in a lighthearted manner, but it resonated. My in-box was jammed that day. Steve Doocy was doing a remote segment about the Navy Sea Chanters, commenting that it had been an all-male group until 1980, when women were allowed to join. On the set with me Brian Kilmeade joked, with faux disapproval, "Women are everywhere. We're letting 'em play golf and tennis now. It's out of control." I stood up and walked off the set, calling back, "You know what, you read the headlines since you're so great. Go ahead, take 'em away."

Brian laughed. "Leaving an all-male crew . . ."

"In all your glory—go for it," I called.

I didn't "storm off" the set, as some reported. I didn't "shout angrily," as others portrayed the moment. The manner was strictly teasing. But I guess I made my point, especially in the eyes of the blogs and journalists who usually don't come out swinging for me. Suddenly they all loved me for standing up for women's rights!

I put myself out there, so I'm fair game. Now that I have my own show, called *The Real Story with Gretchen Carlson,* I hear a lot from my viewers. I often have to laugh when I read my e-mails. A woman writes, "How can you consider yourself a Christian woman with that kind of cleavage?" Then the very next e-mail will be from a man: "Could you please wear that dress every day?" That makes me chuckle. I love my viewers, and I recognize that, like me, they are individuals with their own viewpoints. They are interesting and diverse, and keeping up with them is a big job.

I fight for women to be respected for everything they are and do, and I ask it for myself. We're all complex beings, full of unique gifts and opportunities. I'm blessed to find fulfillment in each of my roles—as a wife and mother of two, as a journalist and anchor of a television show, as a musician, as a woman of faith whose weekly highlight is teaching Sunday school alongside my husband. Like every woman I know, I juggle a full load of both joys and stresses.

In one of those early New York interviews, after I won Miss America, the newsman Jack Cafferty challenged a statement I'd made that I didn't become Miss America because of "luck." My words seemed to offend him. He prodded me: "If you had to say it again, wouldn't you rephrase it?" I think he had the idea that you just walked out on a stage, flashed a pretty smile, twirled, and took your chances. I assured him that luck didn't get me there. I worked my butt off for that opportunity.

We all have some luck in our life, but believe me, I don't tell my children, "Maybe you'll get lucky." I tell them to work hard and study and give it their all. I make sure they understand what it means to have strong values and always strive to do the right thing. Looking back, I remember myself at the age of eleven—my daughter's age. My dream then was to play the violin on a world stage. No one told me I wasn't good enough, or skinny enough, or any other "enough." My life stretched out ahead of me full of possibility, and I lived with the ever-present idea that I could do anything

CHAPTER 1

"Sparkles"

My heart was beating in my throat. My hands felt clammy. Waiting in the wings for my name to be announced, I closed my eyes and repeated the words to the Lord's Prayer once again. At thirteen I was about to give the biggest performance of my life.

The Minnesota Orchestra was onstage at Orchestra Hall playing the rousing piece *Fanfare for the Common Man* by Aaron Copland. The music was fast-paced and uplifting, with trumpets blaring. I was up next to play the first movement of Édouard Lalo's *Symphonie Espagnole*.

When the soundproof doors opened, a rush of cold air came at me and I began the long walk across the stage, violin in hand. I was a chubby girl, awkward in my floor-length white dress, but on that day I was also a concert artist, who would lead an entire orchestra in a performance.

Although it was only 10:30 in the morning, the auditorium was full for the orchestra's popular Coffee Concert. This was a venue for some of the most famous soloists in the country, and today the stage belonged to me. I took my position, fighting nervousness, and everything became silent. The oboe player gave me an A note to tune to. And I began to play.

Just like that, the nervousness fell away and I was lost in the music. I was always a very physical performer, and I poured my heart into interpreting the uplifting Spanish melody. It was not only a matter of technical skill. It was an emotional experience, a feeling of euphoria I've never experienced in any other setting. By the time I was done, my dress was damp with sweat, as if I'd just run a race.

The audience rose to its feet cheering. I heard, "Bravo! Bravo!" The applause seemed to go on forever as I left the stage and returned twice more for encore bows. It was a thrilling moment, and then it was over. Normal life resumed.

Back in the dressing room I changed out of my long white dress, and then my mom drove me to school. I got there in time for math class, where we had a test scheduled. My fellow students didn't even know where I'd been that day. To them I was just one of the kids. They didn't understand the *other* me—the one who had just performed with the Minnesota Orchestra.

That dichotomy was the story of my young life. I was a girl who lived for my music, and I spent much of my time in the hallowed circles of great musicians. But I was also engaged in a constant quest to be a regular kid. It was a sometimes frantic, sometimes confusing double life, and beneath my normally sunny exterior there was a nagging loneliness when I felt that my friends couldn't really know me or be a part of my life with music.

Those two sides of me were in conflict many times over the years. Looking back as an adult, I've come to see that both were a gift of my remarkable upbringing in a small Minnesota town, where exceptionalism and normalcy were valued in equal measure.

From the time I entered the world—almost three weeks late—I made my presence known. I had a big personality as a baby, one that demanded attention. My dad always said that he'd rock me asleep, and the minute he took his hand away my eyes would pop open and I'd start yelling. I believe what they say about personality, that it's there at birth. Mine sure was. I liked having an audience. I was a born ham.

Early entries in my baby book provide clues to my personality:

"Gretchen loves all food and gobbles it down as fast as you can feed her."

"Gretchen talks like crazy."

"Gretchen can turn somersaults!"

Eating, talking, and performing. My most notable characteristics before the age of two. But my personality was more complex than that. I was born on June 21, on the cusp between Cancer and Gemini, and I chose to be a Gemini because I personified the mix of yin and yang. Both outgoing and reserved. Both lighthearted and intense. Both a spitfire and a person who fought for self-confidence. Both a serious musician and a regular kid. The two sides of my personality were on display in everyday life.

I grew up in Anoka, Minnesota, a town that could have come straight out of a snow globe. It's a wonderful little place whose claim to fame is that it's the Halloween Capital of the World. Garrison Keillor is from Anoka, and it was an inspiration for Lake Wobegon, so that gives you an idea.

My parents and both sets of grandparents are of Swedish descent, and Anoka is a town with a heavy Scandinavian influence. When Mom stood on the front porch and called me and my best friend Molly in for lunch, all the schnauzers named Gretchen and the black Labs named Molly came running. From a very early age I knew an important fact about myself: I was 100 percent Swedish. This was a point of pride because even in my small town it wasn't common for people to be 100 percent anything.

My grandpa Hyllengren gave me a nickname that he thought fit a talkative, feisty child. He called me "Sparkles." When he said it in his affectionate tone it came out "Schparkles." I loved that nickname then and I still do. It was a gift from my grandpa, something all my own. I was a short, chubby, willful kid. But to Grandpa I was Sparkles. I used to ask him, "Why do you call me that?" And he'd answer in a soft voice, "It's just the way you are, Schparkles."

Grandpa Hyllengren was a Lutheran minister who grew up in a small farmhouse in Vasa, Minnesota, the son of immigrants from Sweden. His life story is a testament to the value of perseverance, which was embedded in my family story. It was passed on as the theme of my life—to never give up no matter how difficult things were. Grandpa was the fourth of five children and the only one in his family to go to school past the eighth grade. He was determined to go to high school, which was twelve miles away, and after he secured a position as right guard on the football team, he lived with the coach so he could attend. He eventually won a football scholarship to Gustavus Adolphus, a private college in Saint Peter,

Minnesota, that was founded by Swedish immigrants. He played on the football team for four years, but it was the church that called him.

When Grandpa became pastor of Zion Lutheran Church in Anoka, it had 850 members, but under his inspirational leadership it grew to 8,500, becoming the second largest Lutheran church in America. He built his congregation the old-fashioned way, by visiting every new family that moved to Anoka and inviting them to be a member of his church. He told people he was selling insurance for eternal life. He worked incredibly hard and never took a raise.

Grandpa was quite liberal and Grandma was a Republican. We used to ask them why they even bothered voting, since they canceled each other out. But Grandpa never preached politics from the pulpit. He preached about values that transcended political ideas. These were simple homespun messages, using anecdotes from culture and life. To this day I dislike it when a minister preaches politics from the pulpit, and I learned from my grandparents that you could love someone who had different ideas. What a revelation, right? I think we forget that sometimes.

My mother was a high-spirited, outgoing girl, an absolutely beautiful natural blonde. She knew her own mind, and she was very smart. She skipped three grades in elementary school and went to college young. She attended Gustavus Adolphus College, her parents' alma mater, for a year and then transferred to the University of Minnesota. She graduated at age nineteen and became a teacher. Mom had her share of suitors, including the guy she was "pinned" to when she met my father.

The story of my parents' meeting is cute. She was home from college during Christmastime, and her mother was having a tea and had invited people from church and the neighborhood. My father's family lived right down the street and attended Zion, but she had never met Dad because he'd been away in the service. Mom walked into the living room, and standing at the punch bowl was a handsome young man who caught her eye. His name was Lee Carlson. She went right back into the kitchen and told her mother that Lee Carlson was the man she was going to marry. Her mother probably laughed, but you have to know that my mother has always possessed an extreme level of determination. If she set her sights on Lee Carlson, he didn't have a chance.

But my dad played a bit hard to get. That's where my mom's strategizing skills came in—how to get him to ask her out. In the spring she put on her hottest two-piece bathing suit and started lying out in front of the house in a lawn chair just when she knew Lee Carlson would be driving by to go home for lunch. Quite racy for the minister's daughter! Dad would whiz by in his red convertible, and I guess he took notice. He finally asked her out.

At first my grandfather didn't approve of Dad because he thought he'd been born with a silver spoon in his mouth. But he soon came to see what a hard worker Dad was. He worked at Main Motors, the car dealership that had been in his family since 1919. It's one of the oldest family-run businesses in Minnesota, with a storefront showroom on Main Street. It was originally owned by my dad's great-uncle, and he sold Chevrolet cars and trucks, and then added Oldsmobile, Buick, and Cadillac. In 1934, the year my dad was born, his father, LeRoy Carlson, bought the dealership from his uncle.

My dad started pumping gas at the dealership when he was ten years old. Dad did every job, from laboring in the service and parts department to selling cars. "He worked like a slave," my mother once said. No sign of a silver spoon. When his father died in 1966, Dad took over the dealership with his brother.

Dad worked a lot, often returning to the dealership after dinner. Car dealerships are very volatile businesses, closely tied to the state of the economy. If there's a recession, or even a hint of one, sales dry up. The 1970s were an especially difficult time because of the oil crisis.

Family always came first with my parents, and their four children were the center of their lives. My sister, Kris, was first, then two and a half years later I made my entrance, followed by my brothers Bill and Mark. We all had our unique personalities. Kris was a pretty girl with a lovely personality. I always envied her beautiful long hair, because my hair was thin and brittle and when I was young, I wore it in a short shag that was almost boyish. (At one point my mother started getting my hair permed, and trust me, it wasn't a pretty sight.) Unlike Kris, I was a tomboy. I preferred to hang out with my brothers and their friends. We'd congregate and roam around the neighborhood, playing army in the woods or football on the lawn. There was nothing I liked more than to play dodgeball or watch golf and football on TV.

My dad was raised in a traditional Swedish environment of strictness and stoicism, but he ended up being the most sentimental, loving person I know. There wasn't a lot of emotion in his upbringing, but Dad can be a virtual waterworks of emotion, crying at movies, sporting events, and sad or happy stories.

My dad's father was definitely the head of the household while he was alive, but after he died Grandma Vi really came into her own. I knew her as an amazing, independent woman who traveled the world with girlfriends. In my eyes she was a trailblazer. She was also somewhat eccentric, with her own style. She never changed her hairstyle during her whole adult life, wearing it in a short pageboy. She got a kick out of me. Whenever I walked into a room, she'd announce, "Here comes trouble with a capital T."

We also spent a lot of time at Grandpa and Grandma Hyllengren's house and always had fun. Grandpa was a religious man but he had a great bawdy sense of humor. His favorite TV show was *The Benny Hill Show*. He was also a big jokester. We'd beg him to tell jokes, but he never did it on demand. Instead he'd surprise us with one when we were least expecting it. We loved his elaborate schemes. On Easter he would organize a giant Easter egg hunt. He'd hide candy all over his house and then write elaborate clues that were very convoluted. We loved the challenge of figuring out his clues. Grandpa would get frustrated with me always guessing the clues first, so he would announce, "Now, this next one is for everyone *except* Gretchen."

Grandma Hyllengren was a very mild-mannered woman, almost meek, but love poured from her. She was beloved by the congregation, and I always felt that we had a special connection. She wasn't at all like me, but she seemed to understand me and accept me for who I was. I was drawn to her peaceful nature, like a reprieve from my more aggressive spirit—and my mom's too. She had played violin in college, so she was especially proud of me when I started playing "her" instrument. Grandma had never played seriously, but I liked that we shared this bond through the violin.

Grandma Hyllengren was my sounding board. If I had a fight with my mom, I'd get on my bike and go over to her house. We'd bake cookies together and drink Fresca—the only soda my grandparents bought. She'd listen to my woes, and she'd even defend me to my mom. She once said to her, "You can't stop Gretchen from being Gretchen."

My mother was as outgoing as her mother was shy. She was the social force of our family, and the life of the party, with a gregarious nature and a great laugh. She was a terrific cook and loved to entertain, and her parties were popular. Kris and I were enlisted to dress in cute matching outfits and carry around hors d'oeuvres. The guests ate and ate, and we returned to the kitchen many times for refills. Eventually we'd get tired and complain, but Mom would just say, "Get back out there and put a smile on your face," and back we'd go until our trays were empty.

Faith was a constant in our lives. It seemed as if we were always in church. It was the centerpiece of every week, especially on Sundays. Our whole family pitched in. Kris and I sometimes performed for all three services, playing violin, cello, and piano, often in duets. We also sang in the choir, and I taught Sunday school in high school. Mom taught Sunday school and Dad sang in the choir. If I was playing for more than one service, I liked to sit in the sacristy— a little room off the altar. It felt like being at a private club during church, because I'd see Grandpa each time he came back during the service. The church was like a second home to me.

Having Grandpa in the pulpit was like watching a rock star. He was a dynamic and inspirational preacher, and he had an amazing way with people. He made church personal for me. I remember going up to the altar for Communion and kneeling down. He would brush his hand (slightly curled from the arthritis he refused to have treated) softly across my cheek before giving me the bread and grape juice, as if to say, "You're my girl." I still get tears in my eyes thinking about it.

I always say that my wonderful grandfather gave me the gift of faith. He baptized me, married me, and baptized my daughter, Kaia. Sadly, he died just three weeks before my son, Christian, was born. But Grandpa's gift is still alive inside of me. As curious as I am about so many things in the world, the one thing I've never questioned is my faith. No matter what goal I have tried to achieve in life, I've always known that God is right by my side.

In our household, being a Christian was more than going to church on Sunday. We weren't Bible thumpers. We practiced a daily Christianity that was as practical as it was spiritual. My father always told me, "Gretchen, people will know you're a Christian by the way you act." He was a perfect example of that. It was important for him to be a good person in the community. My mom, too. Growing up, I just took it for granted that everyone had warm and charitable hearts. It made me admire my parents even more when I learned how special their kindness was. Mom was a regular volunteer in the church and in the community, participating in Meals on Wheels and making Easter baskets for those in need. Dad belonged to the hospital board and Kiwanis. That spirit of involvement is not as prevalent today. People say they're too busy. But my parents were also busy, running a business and raising four kids. It comes down to priorities—and to caring. People always comment on how nice Minnesotans are. But that niceness is practiced in action. That's the way I was raised.

Today when I speak my mind, the topic is often Christianity. I'm not a "God-clutcher," as William Goldman depicted me. That's not the way I was taught. I was taught to be accepting of our nation's diversity, including its religious diversity. I often get criticized for supposedly not liking people who are atheists. That couldn't be further from the truth. It's a free country. But I feel compelled to speak out when I see society veering off course to an unhealthy extent—on the one hand becoming more tolerant of diversity and on the other hand trying to marginalize Christianity. Sometimes it's downright crazy. Take the recent debate about a cross at the World Trade Center memorial site. When the World Trade Center collapsed, there appeared in the rubble a seventeen-foot cross-shaped beam. That cross wasn't created by people—it was naturally formed in the collapse. A lot of Americans found it comforting. For me it was a sign from God that we can find unity as a nation and a world after a horrendous act of terrorism. But whether you take it that way or just see it as two beams in the rubble, it's a historical artifact. It actually happened that way. I covered Ground Zero as a reporter and saw it for myself. But an organization of atheists challenged a plan to include the cross at the 9/11 Memorial Museum on the basis of its being a Christian symbol. They later lost in court, but I just shake my head in amazement at these kinds of antics. It bothers me that some people express an antipathy to Christianity. The American notion of freedom of religion doesn't preclude celebrating your faith.

I come to these views sincerely after a lifetime of religious practice, but I also want my children to have the opportunity I had to fully celebrate Christianity without its meaning being hijacked by people who don't really give a rip. Rituals and symbols of faith were essential to my life growing up in Minnesota. They anchored the lessons my grandfather preached from the pulpit, and I know they made me a better person, more compassionate and giving.

It was thanks to our religion that we had exposure to the world at large as kids. Every year my grandfather would organize a trip to the Holy Land for his church, and we went to Israel several times. We'd usually combine those trips with visits to other locations, so one year we went to Egypt and another year to Germany.

When we went to Israel, we'd bring packs of gum and pens and pencils to hand out to the kids in poor areas. They'd see us coming, and within a few seconds we'd have a huge crowd around us. Many of them had never seen gum before. The 1970s were a very tense time in the Middle East, and even as young children we were aware of that. When we traveled from Egypt to Israel we went through heavily armed checkpoints and were all searched. The sight of men with rifles everywhere and the sense of constant danger made me appreciate our life back home.

My parents and grandparents often quoted the passage from Luke, "To whom much is given, much is expected." And they showed us the world to give the passage meaning. It became an enduring theme of my life—the idea that I was so blessed and that I had to have high expectations for myself and give back as much as I could.

Even as a child, I tried to stand up for myself. I was an early reader, and my mom will tell you that she doesn't even know how I learned to read so young. But by the time I went to kindergarten in the fall, I was quite good. On the first day of school our teacher, Mrs. Grosslein, divided the class into kids who could read and kids who couldn't, and she put me in the group of kids who couldn't read. All morning I kept raising my hand, saying, "But Mrs. Grosslein, I know how to read." And she'd tell me to keep quiet. Finally I went up to her desk and cried, very upset, "Mrs. Grosslein, I know how to read!"

She hushed me and said, "No, no, we'll just keep you where you are."

I ran all the way home crying and slammed the door behind me, screaming, "I know how to read! I know how to read!"

I can still remember the agony of that experience—being able to do something and being told you couldn't. My intense reaction was a precursor to the way I always pushed myself to achieve. I never wanted to be told I couldn't accomplish something. So in a way, maybe I have Mrs. Grosslein partly to thank for some of my later fiery determination.

My best friend growing up—and to this day—was Molly Kinney, who lived ten houses away. We both lived on the Mississippi River. Her father was a doctor and she was one of six kids. We became best friends in first grade after we both showed up for the school photo wearing the exact same blue-and-white dress.

Like I said, I was chubby as a kid. Molly was skinny. My mom used to keep our kitchen stocked with all kinds of goodies, although she always had her eye on me. "Do not touch those doughnuts," she'd warn. Then she'd leave the house and Molly and I would sneak in and eat a few doughnuts. When my mom came home and saw they were missing, I'd blame Molly—and Molly always went along with it. I was happy about that. The only problem is, I kept getting fatter and Molly kept getting skinnier.

I just loved doughnuts and pastry. Hans Bakery was right on the way to school, and I'd stop and get a doughnut or an elephant ear, a puff pastry confection, huge and flat in the shape of an elephant's ear, flaky and sweet.

At the time I was a huge fan of Fran Tarkenton, the famous Vikings quarterback. I knew he didn't sign many autographs, but when we went to Vikings games I'd wait in the parking lot in my snowsuit, hoping for a chance. One Sunday as dozens of us were swarming around Tarkenton and his car, he announced, pointing at me, "I'll do one more autograph—for the chubby little girl with the pigtails." I was ecstatic and didn't even care that he called me chubby because I had his autograph—and still do. I've interviewed Tarkenton several times on Fox, and we always chuckle at the autograph story.

My mom had me on a diet constantly. She instructed my babysitter, future congresswoman Michele Bachmann (who was Michele Amble at the time), not to let me drink any sugary sodas, but Michele did anyway, and I loved her for that. Michele had long, straight brown hair, which I envied. Many years later she joked in an interview, "It was my Cher period."

Our house was right on the Mississippi River, which made for a glorious childhood. We had wonderful times boating, but there was always a sense of danger because the current was swift. We were warned about how Grandpa's brother had drowned in a river in southern Minnesota when he was in his early twenties. But we'd go out as a family on a big pontoon, stopping at small islands to eat picnic lunches. Sometimes Dad would let us float along in inner tubes while he followed us in the boat. Sometimes we fished. I was proud of being able to bait a hook and fish all on my own. We also dug for clams and hunted for agates. Agates were almost impossible to find—like a needle in a haystack. It was a huge sense of accomplishment to find one. We made many happy memories during those summers. Today I love sharing those simple pleasures with my kids, and take them back to Minnesota to do that—preferably in the summertime when it's not twenty below zero! We water-ski, look for agates, and go horseback riding and fishing. Making s'mores and playing bingo are just as fulfilling, if not more so, than playing games on an iPad.

Anoka was small, but in terms of family and community it was huge. All my relatives lived less than a mile away. My parents knew everyone. We'd have big potluck suppers at the church, and everyone would bring a dish—meatballs, tuna casserole, Jell-O—simple foods. I remember that every person got accolades for their dish, and people glowed with the praise. It was a warm experience of extended family. When I talked in the Miss America pageant about growing up with values, I meant it not as an abstract idea but as a real-life experience that was embedded in my upbringing.

Of course, being Swedish was a big deal growing up. My grandparents still spoke Swedish to each other, especially when they didn't want the kids to understand what they were saying. I loved the lilting sound of the language. I always felt proud to have this heritage that was *me* right down to the genes. It was something no one could ever take away. Our lives were influenced in many ways by Swedish culture, but mostly it was the food, especially around the Christmas holidays. That's when you knew you were Swedish!

Maybe the one time it wasn't so great was when the lutefisk dinners started cropping up on the family schedule. In Minnesota, you can find a lutefisk dinner every night of the week in December at some area church. Lutefisk is a Swedish "delicacy" that you can only get at a butcher shop around Christmastime. It's actually cod, except that they soak it in lye for several days—that's right, lye.

The stuff you make soap with. My mom bought it at the butcher's shop and kept it in the garage until Christmas Eve. Number one, to keep it cold. Number two, because it stunk so bad there wasn't enough Lysol on the planet to deodorize the refrigerator once the lutefisk had been inside. It had to be baked in a foil pan because it would blacken any real dish. When it came out, it wobbled on the plate like jellyfish, with the bones still in it. We'd douse it in melted butter and a gluelike white sauce—all to try to hide the taste. By high school I had finally acquired a taste for it—kind of.

My mom always cooked Christmas Eve dinner for the whole family because Grandpa and Grandma Hyllengren were so busy at church. Meatballs with a light brown gravy, mashed potatoes, pickled herring, broccoli mold with a creamy mushroom sauce over the top, cooked carrots, lutefisk, and of course, lefse, a soft potato pancake cooked thin like a crepe. You'd roll it up and put butter and sugar in it. For dessert there was an impressive display of cookies: frosted roll-out cookies in Christmas shapes that we would help make (messy!); cinnamon thumbs; green cornflake wreaths with two cinnamon candies as the ribbon; krumkake, a rolled waffle cookie; and spritz with jelly filling. The adults drank glögg out of mugs. It was a very potent concoction of spiced wine and spirits.

After we ate and before we opened presents, we performed our own Christmas pageant. We'd play Christmas carols on our instruments, and then we'd do a Nativity play where we'd take turns playing Mary, Joseph, and the shepherds. (Baby Jesus was a doll.) We were tired and overexcited by that point, so inevitably a fight would break out and someone would end up running crying to their room. Then my parents would have to settle us down and bring us back together to open presents. We opened presents from each other on Christmas Eve and presents from Santa on Christmas morning. Presents from Santa were never wrapped, and years later I figured out why. There was no way my parents could get it all done with cooking the food, driving us back and forth to services, and Dad returning to sing in the choir for the 11:00 p.m. service. I've kept the tradition of not wrapping Santa's gifts. I love how it saves time!

In spite of the tears, I also came to treasure the tradition of a Christmas Eve program at home, and still do it with my family every year. Like all children, my kids are not so enthusiastic— they want to get to the presents. But it's a lovely tradition, and one I know they'll remember as meaningful their whole lives.

If faith was the centerpiece of our lives, music was a close second. My mom played the piano. My dad sang in the church choir and did solos. He had a beautiful voice, and he also played the piccolo and the flute. My grandmother played the violin. Eventually all four of us kids learned musical instruments. Kris played the cello, and my brothers played trumpet and saxophone. Even as a very little girl, I sat at the piano and plunked on the keys. (Ironically, my grandfather had no musical talent whatsoever. Sometimes when he was officiating at a service, he'd forget to turn off his microphone, and the whole congregation could hear him sing. It was awful, but also funny.) When I was six, I begged my parents to let me learn to play the piano. That was fine with them because they believed that learning to play an instrument was a good way for kids to develop confidence and self-discipline.

My parents took me to a piano teacher who lived just up the

road. She took one look at my hands and said, "I'm sorry, but Gretchen will never be a good piano player. Her hands are just too small." I was so disappointed I almost started crying. She suggested we go up to Fred Moore Junior High School and see if I could find another instrument. My dad took me because my mom was under the weather that day (a rare occurrence for her). The music teacher, Ken Davenport, looked around and by pure chance handed me a violin. I was thrilled—although the violin was almost as big as me. When I got home with my big new violin I ran up to Mom's bedroom to show her. I was beyond excited, but the instrument really was too big for me. Soon after, Mr. Davenport found a quarter-size violin that was just the right size.

Someone once said that finding the right instrument is like falling in love. That's exactly what happened to me. The first time my fingers slid along the strings, I felt an emotional charge, a happiness that was new and exciting. My parents asked Mr. Davenport if he would teach me, and at first he wasn't sure he had the time. He put them off, saying, "We'll see." But when they took me over to play with him one day, he couldn't let me go. He kept saying, "Just a little longer." He was taken with me, just as I was taken with the violin. He finally agreed to work with me, but he told my parents, "She's going to outgrow me before long." I started going for lessons every Monday, Wednesday, and Friday.

I was full to the brim in my love of music. It felt familiar and right to me—a way to express my personality and emotions that was uniquely my own and that I could control. I mastered the basics very quickly, in part because I was able to sight-read the music, which is a gift. I was bursting with confidence, wanting to play for people every chance I got.

After I'd been playing for three months, as the Christmas season approached, I boldly went up to our church choir director, Donna Legrid. "Can I play violin with the choir?" I asked.

She looked down at me in surprise. "Didn't you just start playing?"

"Yes," I said with my six-year-old bravado, "but I know how to play."

So I played "Are You Weary, Little Donkey?" with the church choir for the Christmas services. That Christmas I also made my first recording—a cassette of Christmas carols for my dad, with my mom accompanying me on the piano.

I had been studying with Mr. Davenport for only a few months when he took me to play for his junior high orchestra. I'm sure it was not a pleasant experience for the students to have a little girl held up to them as an example. They probably thought, "Who is this squirt showing us up?" When Mr. Davenport told them that I was going to be a guest soloist at their concert, I doubt if they were so happy, but I was oblivious. I was just excited about playing for an audience. I performed a Handel sonata, third and fourth movements, on my little violin. And the applause thrilled me.

About that time Mr. Davenport had me start studying with his daughter, Jeanette Simmons, who was a violinist. But it was becoming clear to him that I was progressing fast and needed a higher level of training. He got in touch with a friend who was a professional musician and arranged for me to see him to get his opinion. I didn't know it at the time, but this would be an important turning point in my budding musical career.

CHAPTER 2

Little Girl in a Big Orchestra

The Flame Room was the best nightclub in Minneapolis. Set in the elegant Radisson Hotel, the Flame Room was meant to evoke an intimate New York City nightclub. This was the place where some of the greatest performers in America had played over the years— including Peggy Lee, Milton Berle, Sid Caesar, and Phyllis Diller. Nat King Cole once stopped by to perform with the house orchestra, the Golden Strings. Presidents and dignitaries visited the club, which was packed every night of the week.

And there I was. It was late evening, and the flickering candlelight bounced off of the flocked red tapestry wallpaper. I walked in from the lobby of the hotel, wearing a pretty dress with white tights, clutching my small violin case. I was seven years old.

Actually, it wasn't the first time I'd been to the Flame Room.

My family used to go to dinner there a couple times a year for fun. That's where I first saw my uncle eat raw oysters, throwing his head back and swallowing them whole. I thought it was gross, but it made an impression on me. I remember too being mesmerized by the flaming entrees.

That night I was there with my parents and Ken Davenport, to play the violin for a very important person. Cliff Brunzell, who was known as a violin firebrand, had performed in the Minnesota Orchestra before he gave it up in the 1960s to lead the Golden Strings at the Flame Room. They were playing a lively jazz number as we came in the door, and I barely had time to glance at the stage before we were led through an entryway to a back room where we waited for Mr. Brunzell to finish his set. Mr. Davenport had asked him to listen to me play, and he'd agreed.

As we sat waiting, the music stopped, and moments later Mr. Brunzell swept into the room. He was tall and handsome, with a head of thick dark hair and a friendly smile.

He greeted me warmly. "Hello, young lady, I hear you're going to play for me," he said, with what seemed like genuine anticipation.

I grinned and stepped forward. At that time I didn't know enough to be nervous or afraid. I'd been practicing my Bach Concerto in A minor with Mr. Davenport and Jeanette, and I was always happy to play for an audience.

Mr. Davenport motioned me to begin and I started to play, swept up in the music and feeling totally unselfconscious. I was vaguely aware that others from Brunzell's string band began to fill the doorway listening. When I finished, everyone applauded, my mom hugged me, and I stood there grinning.

"How long have you been playing, Gretchen?" Brunzell asked.

"Almost a year," I said proudly. "I'm in the second grade."

"I see." He studied me thoughtfully as Mr. Davenport explained that I had already surpassed his ability to teach me. I needed a higher level of instruction.

"Take her to Mary West," Brunzell said. "She's the best."

Before I left, Brunzell bent down and shook my hand. "It's always a pleasure to hear another artist at work," he said. I glowed. I was an artist!

Everyone told me that auditioning for Mary West was a big deal, as she was considered the top violin teacher in Minnesota. She taught at the University of Minnesota MacPhail Center for Music, in addition to having private students, and she was very choosy about her private students. I went to the university to audition for her. About a hundred students were crammed into the room when I auditioned. I played "Flight of the Bumblebee," which is a very fast piece. Everyone clapped wildly, and Mary told my parents that she'd take me on as a private student.

Mary West would become the pivotal person in my life. She was a small, motherly woman of sixty, with big glasses and reddish brown hair that she didn't wear in any particular style. She always wore comfortable clothes, like polyester pants with a long sweater and a big necklace. She was soft-spoken and very warm. Her big beaming smile gave me confidence.

I learned that before she married and settled down in Minnesota, Mary and her twin sister, Virginia, had been quite well known as the Drane Sisters, a traveling musical act. They even performed at the White House for Franklin and Eleanor Roosevelt in 1938. But as Mary told me many times, she was a much better teacher than a performer. Teaching was her calling, and she would continue doing so until 2007, when she died at the age of ninety-seven, leaving behind thousands of devoted students who had been blessed to know her.

Mary had a gift for working with young children. She could spot potential and she knew how to nurture it in the youngest of us. In the hard-driven and competitive world of music, she was unfailingly gentle and encouraging. She had boundless patience, and in all the time I studied with her she never yelled at me or got frustrated. If I screwed up, she'd say softly, "It's okay, baby. It'll be better next time." Her loving attention motivated me. She wanted to bring out the best in me, and I wanted to *be* the best to please her. I loved seeing her eyes light up when I played well. She was joyful, and being with her filled me with joy. Today, when I talk to other parents about how to motivate kids, I always think of Mary. Some people believe that the way to instill discipline and excellence is to be tough and uncompromising—to motivate through fear. I was blessed to have experienced another way. Through Mary, I learned that the greatest way to inspire young children is to tell them you believe in them and to make them feel as if they are the most special person in the world. When I was working with Mary, I always thought I was her favorite student, and I later heard from other students that they thought *they* were her favorites as well.

Every Friday morning, instead of going to school, my mom drove me to Mary's house in an old neighborhood in South Minneapolis, along back roads. The trip took an hour and a half. When we entered the house, Mary always greeted me with a kiss—"How're you doing, baby doll?"—and I would tussle with her dog, Maggie, for a few minutes. Maggie was a friendly black-and-white mutt who looked as if she hadn't been brushed in years. Her messy appearance fit right in with the messiness of the house.

We practiced in a small study. The room was filled with piles of books and stacks of music. There was a piano squeezed against the wall and a music stand, with just enough room for Mary and me to stand during practice. It was a tight fit. Mom would sit a few inches away and take notes in her beautiful penmanship:

"Watch your bow arm."

"Don't tug the bow too hard with your index finger."

"Intonation problems on the fast part of page three."

"Lift your chin."

"Practice this passage twenty times."

Our lessons normally started with exercises. As I accomplished each one to Mary's satisfaction, she checked the page and assigned a new one.

She marked my music with a thick pencil, which had a dark texture that smudged on the page. I loved those pencils. They had removable square erasers on the end, and because I was such a perfectionist I would use those erasers a lot when I wrote notes myself.

Even as a seven-year-old I could tell that Mary was kind of eccentric. There were photos in the house of her and her sister performing in the most glamorous gowns imaginable. But Mary had left glamour behind. Now she and her husband, Bob, and their three children lived a different kind of life, which I thought of as artsy. Mary and Bob were crazy about each other, totally devoted, and it felt good to be in their presence. Bob wrote his wife love poems and bought her bouquets of flowers. Their house was like no other place I'd ever been. My mother was meticulous, with everything in its place. Mary's house was like a storm—books and junk everywhere. The rooms were narrow and dark, with a steep staircase up to the attic, where I never dared to go, and another one down to the basement where a boarder lived. I never met the boarder.

Bob was a freelance journalist and he was home a lot. He had an electric dump truck track set up on the dining room table. The truck would go around the track, up and down hills, dumping its load into barrels. He'd show me all the switches and features, and I loved watching that dump truck go around the track.

Bob could also play the nose flute, which delighted me no end. It was a semi-plastic device that he put on his nose. He'd blow into it and play a song. I always laughed and clapped. Bob was fun.

The lessons lasted two hours, and halfway through we'd take a break and have a snack. Bob would appear in the doorway. "Can I make you my tuna special?" he'd ask with a flourish. Of course! Bob was the cook in the family, and he made the best tuna sandwich I'd ever had—oil-packed tuna with lots of mayonnaise on toast—and I really looked forward to it.

"Half," Mom said.

"Whole!" I argued.

Sometimes I got half a sandwich like Mom wanted, and sometimes I got a whole. I loved to eat, but Mom was always watching my waistline.

In spite of dietary restrictions, Mom and I had another ritual after the lesson. We stopped at Dairy Queen on the way home. I always got a vanilla cone with sprinkles on top, and this was before lunch!

Over the months and years to come, Mary took me through a classical training repertoire, beginning with the easiest—Bach, Vivaldi—then on to Handel and Mozart and Mendelssohn. And eventually to Tchaikovsky, Paganini, Brahms, and Beethoven. Beethoven wasn't hard because of the notes but because of the interpretation. You had to be a mature player to interpret Beethoven.

Standing in Mary's cramped music room, with my violin pressed against my chin and my fingers dancing through the notes, I was transported into another world—one where I wasn't a little kid but a performer who could bring the most wondrous melodies to life. It was pure joy. The ability to play music gave me a depth well beyond my years. At seven years old, I lacked the vocabulary to express my feelings, but music placed a rich vocabulary at my disposal every single day. I remember thinking, "This is mine . . . this beauty belongs to me, and nothing can change it." Big emotions for a little girl.

My first recital for Mary was held at the MacPhail Center for Music in June 1974, just as I finished second grade. I played Bach's Concerto in A minor, first movement. I was accompanied on the piano by a woman named Thelma Johnson, who would become my piano accompanist for many years. Thelma was a warmhearted redhead, and she was a lot of fun to be around. Her husband played bass for the Minnesota Orchestra. Their kids were grown, and I think Thelma just loved having me around. It sounds funny to say that she became my friend, since she was an adult and I was a little girl, but I didn't have any real music friends then, so that's what happened.

Sometimes I'd stay over at Thelma's house. She had three pianos, and we played together and laughed our heads off. In spite of the warning that my hands were too small for piano, I studied it on the side with a local teacher for years just for fun, and I thought of it as my escape. Unlike the violin, which always came with a certain amount of performance stress, the piano was just pure entertainment, and it's still fun for me today.

Thelma played for me at every recital and every competition and audition. Later, she played at my wedding. She's still alive and quite elderly, and I've seen her from time to time over the years. I once took my daughter, Kaia, to play the piano for her, and it was a very happy visit, one Kaia remembers fondly.

Through it all, my mother was my ballast, my shelter from any storm. She always told me, even when I was a very small child, "Gretchen, you can be anything you want to be." But she also said, "God gave you talents and He expects you to make the most of them."

I've thought of my mother's words many times during my life. I had friends whose mothers didn't encourage them or challenge them in this way, and I think it's so important for children to know that their parents trust them to succeed and that the world is open to them.

I think if it had been up to my dad, he wouldn't have pushed me so hard to pursue music seriously. But even though he was the musician in the family, Mom was much more mindful that my talent was not something to fool around with. She certainly wasn't a "stage mom" in the typical way. But she made a tremendous commitment on my behalf. I always felt very lucky, and we had a special closeness formed over years of mutual effort. I also think that my mother was an incredibly bright and passionate person, but she never capitalized on it for herself. She channeled her talent into helping her kids, and I was the beneficiary of that. My fondest memories are of driving to performances with my mom—just the two of us in the car. I was always anxious and I didn't want to talk, but she'd chatter anyway, giving me a pep talk, putting me at ease.

My father, a great lover of music, with an impeccable ear, gave me a different kind of support. He performed a ritual with me before every concert or audition. In our living room I would do a mock performance with only one audience member—Dad. I'd play the entire piece, and he would lean back in his chair, eyes closed and a faint smile on his lips, really listening. I knew he heard every note, every little nuance. He always gave me an honest appraisal. I needed that ritual, but it wasn't easy. For me it was much easier to play before five thousand people than it was to stand in the living room and play for my father. When my dad said I was ready to go, I was ready to go.

I loved playing for recitals and at church, and I had some pretty remarkable experiences along the way. My first great opportunity was being chosen to play for Isaac Stern. I was ten years old. Stern was doing what he called "A Conversation About the Fiddle" at Macalester College. Three students were selected to play for him, and I was one of them. The other two were older than me, as usual, and one of them was a violin major at Juilliard.

I was the first to play. Thelma sat at the piano, with Mary standing a few feet away looking on with pride. I stood next to Thelma, waiting to begin. Isaac Stern came bounding out, a big round man who seemed to fill the whole stage with his energy. He gave me a warm smile and seemed delighted by me, a little ten-year-old. So I played for him, the first movement and cadenza of the Mozart Concerto in G. When I finished, he clapped enthusiastically. Then he came over and bent down and took my face in his hands. I was waiting for his critique, because that's why we were there. He looked into my eyes and told me, "You need to do only one thing. Grow up and get an adult-size violin." Then he turned to the audience and said, "This child is a credit to her parents. Are they here?" My parents stood, beaming with pleasure at the praise.

Mary was proud of me that day, and we all understood what Isaac Stern meant by growing into an adult violin. I was playing a half-size at that point, and the small violins just didn't have the power or resonance. Nobody spent too much money on them, because you'd just grow out of them. It was a little frustrating, because the reviews at competitions were often along the lines of, "We can tell you have an incredible sound, we just can't hear it." There was only so much you could pull out of a quarter-size or half-size violin. So I had to be patient and wait for my arms to grow.

I won't say the instrument was everything, but it was a big thing. If two people at the same level were playing, you'd always choose the one with the better instrument. When I reached the point of choosing an adult violin around age thirteen, I tested about twenty-five models before I made my decision. It was a very personal choice. Someone once said it was as important as choosing a husband. I still have that instrument, and it's one of my most cherished possessions.

The summer I was eleven, Mary, Bob, and their children took off for three months to stay at a camping resort in Maine. It was impossible for me to be without a teacher for three months, so that's when the idea came for me to audition for a place at the Aspen Music Festival. I didn't realize at the time that it was rare for a child my age to go to Aspen. It would start a whole new chapter in my life.

Dorothy DeLay was considered by many people to be the greatest violin teacher in the country. She taught at Juilliard, as well as directing the Aspen Music Festival. When I went to audition for her I felt intimidated. She was a very large and imposing woman, with a red wig and a shapeless blue dress with a colored scarf. She didn't treat me with the warmth and deference I was used to receiving from Mary. She was strictly business, with an impatient attitude that said, "Don't waste my time. Show me what you've got." And I did. I was many years younger than most of the other artists who would be at the festival—most were in their twenties—but I passed muster with Miss DeLay and was accepted into the program.

That first year I only went for four of the nine weeks. It began as a vacation. While Dad stayed behind to run the car dealership, Mom and I and my siblings piled into a van with Mom's friend Andrea and her daughter Kristin, who was my sister's age. We wound our way west, stopping at Mount Rushmore and Bear Country in South Dakota. It was an adventure, although the long ride was tough on me because I had always suffered from carsickness. I survived by chewing roll after roll of Tums, to the point that my brothers nicknamed me "Mother Tums." In retrospect, my roiling stomach might have been caused by nerves, because while everyone else was having fun, I was going to Aspen to work, and I had no idea what I would encounter. With each mile, my body was telling me I was facing the unknown.

We rented a condo called Aspen Square in the middle of the village of Aspen. It featured a Baskin-Robbins on the ground floor and a beautiful pool that I was allowed to use when I wasn't practicing.

In 1978, Aspen was not the glamorous, celebrity-driven place it is today. There was no Chanel store, no Ritz-Carlton, and no McDonald's. The people were very down-to-earth, and the clothes and food reflected that. Many people were vegetarians, which wasn't that common then, and they were very health conscious. No cars were allowed in the center of town, which featured cobblestone streets with shops and restaurants lining the way. There was an aluminum hut at the end of the cobblestone mall that sold giant chocolate chip cookies hot out of the oven. To this day I've never tasted a better chocolate chip cookie.

The first hurdle was an audition to determine where I would be placed in a summer orchestra. The audition was very intimidating. I entered the room and stood before a panel of judges seated behind a table. The leader was Jorge Mester, the conductor of the Aspen Music Festival. He asked me to play something from Mendelssohn's Concerto in E minor and then he gave me a piece of music to sight-read. This was important because during the festival we had to learn music very quickly to be ready for our performances. He gave us the tempo, then called, "Go!" Since I was a good sight reader, I nailed it. I'm sure this was the reason I was assigned to the Concert Orchestra.

In all there were five orchestras, and the Concert Orchestra was considered the third best—quite an achievement for a first-timer. I sat in the first violin section and my stand partner was David Kim, a fifteen-year-old Asian kid. David and I became good friends that summer and we met up each year. David had been playing the violin since he was three; he went on to become the concertmaster of the Philadelphia Orchestra, and he plays all over the world. That summer we bonded over our youth. We were even boyfriend and girlfriend for a while, in an innocent way. I remember that my family invited David along when we went to eat at the Chart House, my favorite restaurant in Aspen, which had an endless salad bar, great seafood like crab legs in drawn butter, and a rich mud pie dessert. When the waiter asked David if he knew what he wanted, he replied, "Yes, sir, I have my heart set on scallops." My brothers howled with laugher, but I got it. In that setting, fifteen-year-old David wasn't a kid. He was an earnest little adult.

The orchestra met for rehearsal every day and performed each week in "the Tent," a huge outdoor concert hall at the foot of the mountain, with a white canopy over the seats. I can still remember the way the wind would whip up during concerts, slapping the canopy in tune with the music. Summer storms rose up frequently in Aspen, and sometimes there would be a sudden downpour as we were playing—which I found exhilarating. It was a new experience for me to play classical music in a setting of such natural wonder.

Our audience included people from around the world who came to the festival to see some of the best musicians perform. They would bring picnic lunches and dinners and sit on the grass enjoying the music. It was the antithesis of the formal concert hall environment.

At Aspen I learned what it meant to be part of an orchestra, to play as a team effort. I was used to standing out, but now the goal was to blend with the other violinists. So I took my place in the section, a small splash of blonde hair and color amid the more adult artists. My mother used to say I was a little girl in a big orchestra.

After my first summer of just four weeks I returned the next year for the full nine-week program. My mother and brothers accompanied me, but my sister decided to stay home with Dad. My brothers were excited to learn that the actor Steve Martin lived next door. I swear we saw him take out the garbage one morning. That was a highlight.

Mostly what I remember about that summer was the loneliness. My mother drove me to the rehearsals, and nobody really wanted to talk to me—what twenty-year-old wants to hang out with a twelve-year-old? When the orchestra took breaks, I'd sometimes go out front and sit on a huge rock and cry. On one hand I was glad to be there, and when I was playing I was fine, but I was so lonely and out of place. I felt sorry for myself.

The gloom lifted in the middle of the summer when my sister and Molly visited for a week, along with my grandparents, while Mom and my brothers went home for a week. It was wonderful having Molly and Kris there. For once I wasn't lonely. I could see Aspen through their eyes as a wonderful adventure, a time to push the limits. Molly and I went shopping and Molly bought a bright yellow dress that laced up the back. She was slender and lovely, and I was a little bit jealous because I was too chunky to wear the sleek fashions. We were trying to look more mature, and Kris, Molly, and I hatched a scheme to go to a bar one night—as if two twelve-year-olds and a fourteen-year-old could pass for adults. We did go to a bar, but we were too chicken to order a drink.

Playing with a big orchestra was a challenge, but my parents had taught me about mental preparation, which is something I'm not sure a lot of parents do. That simple ritual of performing for my father in the living room readied me mentally for the big stage. My mother's daily pep talks allowed me to curb my performance fears. This support gave me strength in pressure-filled situations for the rest of my life. It was invaluable as I entered my teen years and began being anxious before performances. It's a funny thing. In the early years I was never nervous. I just bounced onto the stage and started playing. But after people kept asking, "Aren't you nervous playing in front of all those people?" I began to think I should be nervous, and then I was. So the mental preparation was absolutely essential. The funny thing is, no matter how nervous I was before a performance, the minute I started playing I felt completely at ease. It's the same way I feel decades later when the red light on the camera signals that I'm on the air. I relax into the role.

Back in Minnesota during the school year, my life was pretty regimented. I got up at 6:00 a.m. every day to get in some practicing before school. Home at 2:30, and more practicing, plus homework and chores. Believe it or not, in spite of all my music work, I had a pretty normal childhood. I was interested in so many things—I didn't want to miss out.

I did have to make some sacrifices because of my practice schedule, which was only natural. I wasn't able to join Girl Scouts or be a crossing guard at school (which I really wanted to do!). I could never hold a knife in the kitchen or chop vegetables or any other normal thing, because it was too easy to slice off the end of a finger.

Molly had started playing the cello, and she and I began playing in a quartet with two other girls, under the direction of Mr. Davenport. We practiced every Monday night for years, and soon were playing at events in the community. Our favorite piece was "I Got Rhythm." Sometimes Mr. Davenport would be our guest artist, playing on the bass a snappy, jazzy version he'd created.

We also played softball for a team called the Lincoln Logs. My mom was the coach, and to this day it amazes me that she let me join the team, with relatively little fear that I would damage my precious hands. I played second base and Molly played first. She was the real athlete and an exceptional hitter. I was envious of how Molly looked in her jeans. Levi's were the rage then, especially light blue cords. I remember taking a ballpoint pen and crossing out the size on my pants label so nobody would know how big my pants were.

By junior high I was becoming conscious of my weight in an unpleasant way. To this day I remember my dread when we competed in the annual 440 race at school, which was part of the President's Fitness Challenge. We had to run around the football field four times, and I agonized over the event for weeks in advance. I couldn't even sleep because I was so worried about it. I hated to run, and my weight held me back. My greatest fear was that I would be dead last, or, worse still, that I wouldn't be able to finish.

I guess maybe I could have skipped going to Hans Bakery on the way to school. I could have chosen not to have doughnuts every day, but I didn't. So I suffered with my fear. I don't think I ever came in last, but the anxiety alone nearly did me in. I wanted to be slimmer and in better shape, but I just didn't care enough to do it at that point in my life.

I was quite sociable, even popular. Because I had so many interests, I was friends with different kinds of people. I didn't fit the stereotype of kids in music or art or sports hanging out in their own cliques. Dad always taught us to be inclusive of everyone, and I took it to heart. I was also very interested in boys, and from the fourth grade on I always had a "boyfriend"—and at that age, my weight didn't seem to be a factor. For me, boys represented fun and an escape from the discipline of practicing.

Molly and I spent a lot of time plotting about boys, and usually we didn't like the same ones, which was a good thing. We spent endless hours over at Molly's house, sitting on her parents' bed and strategizing how to call boys and tell them that we liked them. Finally, after mustering up the courage, Molly would call the boy I liked, and she'd blurt out, "Gretchen likes you. Do you like her?" I'd do the same for her.

On Saturday afternoons we'd go to the roller-skating rink, called Cheapskate, which was also a great place to meet boys. They had a dance called the Snowball. The boys lined up on one side of the rink and the girls on the other. The boys came over and chose a girl they wanted to slow-skate with as a romantic song played. Then the whistle blew and everyone had to find new partners. Ordinarily, I wouldn't have liked being on the spot that way, worried about not being chosen. Luckily, Tom Schultz, my junior high boyfriend, was a great roller skater. He always picked me first.

My friends and I engaged in the normal junior high experimentation. For a while I was hosting "makeout" parties in my parents' basement. That's where we practiced kissing. My house had a little room under the stairs that was a haven in the event of a tornado. There was a single light bulb. We'd cram four couples in, count to three, turn off the light, and everyone would start kissing. Then we'd stop and turn the light back on. It was silly and kind of sweet, and it was also very daring on my part, because if my mom caught wind of what was going on downstairs I would have been in big trouble.

But I was only willing to go so far. Once at a make-out party a boy put his hand up the back of my shirt, and I was outraged. Always one to stand up for myself, I announced to the other girls, "We're leaving!" We got on our bikes and rode single file down the street, with me yelling indignantly, "He put his hand up my shirt!" as if that was the most unthinkable infraction.

During the school year I continued to work with Mary and perform in many recitals. I regularly won competitions, and I got used to seeing my name and picture in the local newspaper. I came to expect it. Then a boy named Gary Levinson came to town, and the competition heated up. Gary was my age and had just moved to Minnesota from Russia, where he'd been playing the violin since he was four. He became my main challenger, and it was like the battle of the violins when Gary and I played. Earlier I described playing as a soloist with the Minnesota Orchestra. That opportunity was the prize for winning the Young People's Symphony Concert Association competition. Gary and I went head-to-head, and when the judges couldn't decide between us, we were both given first prize in a tie. We soloed with the Minnesota Orchestra on separate occasions the following year. Gary went on to have an important musical career and is currently the artistic director of the Chamber Music Society of Fort Worth. We never became friends as children, but I've followed his career with interest. Without knowing it, he had a big influence on my competitive spirit back in Minnesota.

I also competed against Joshua Bell at the 1981 national competition for the American String Teachers Association, which was held in Minnesota. My mother said I played absolutely beautifully, and she figured I'd win the grand prize. Instead, I was first runner-up to Joshua, a kid from Indiana we'd never heard of before. Joshua chose a life in music and became one of the most famous concert violinists in the world. I chose another path, yet our lives have intersected often—an example of the way things come full circle.

Joshua has been on my show many times, and in 2013 I enlisted him as a judge at the Miss America pageant.

I was very serious about my music, but practicing was a grind, and if I had an excuse to skip practice I took it. When I was in the sixth grade I broke the pinky finger of my violin hand playing football. I caught a pass and it bent my finger the wrong way and broke the knuckle. Honestly, I was thrilled. An escape from violin practice! When I ran to tell my mother, she looked at it and said it was nothing. So I kept playing violin, and I was also playing the piano at that time. My piano teacher took one look at my swollen finger and said, "Gretchen, your finger is broken!" Sure enough, we went to a doctor and he put it in a cast. I was elated. I would have to stop practicing until it healed.

In spite of my social nature, I'm struck looking back by how much time I spent by myself. Practicing the violin is mostly a solitary endeavor. At school I was deemed too professional to practice with the other kids, so they put me in a soundproof room so I could work on my own. Often I'd sit in that room and I wouldn't play. It felt like a jail cell. And when I came home from school I was supposed to practice more, and if my mom wasn't home—she was often with my brother at tennis practice—I'd sometimes take a break. My tiny rebellion.

In a study of child prodigies, David Henry Feldman of Tufts University wrote, "If you have a child who is in the world to play the violin, and you decide this child is not going to learn to play the violin— you have killed that child, if not physically, then certainly emotionally and spiritually." In my parents' eyes I was a prodigy, and they felt an obligation to see that my talent was nurtured. The violin was my identity—it was my soul—and my parents were very sensitive to the importance of developing my gift. When Dorothy DeLay told them that I should move to New York and study at Juilliard, my parents felt they had to give the idea serious consideration. After two summers playing at the Aspen Music Festival, Miss De-Lay believed that I could flourish at Juilliard, which would mean uprooting me from my life in Minnesota. My parents agreed to take me to New York for an audition. The idea that this might be the next step on my journey filled me with a mixture of excitement and dread.

I passed the audition, but my feelings were mixed. I wondered if I really wanted to do this, and if my parents were actually thinking of sending me away to live on my own in New York. Was I psychologically ready for such a big step? Were they ready to let me go? I loved music, but I also wanted to fit in. I didn't just want to be "the violin girl." When my parents decided I would stay in Minnesota during the school year to maintain a sense of normalcy and then study with Dorothy DeLay at Aspen during the summers, I was relieved, and later when I understood things better, I was grateful that Mom and Dad didn't ship me off to Juilliard, essentially robbing me of any chance for a childhood.

The next summer my parents allowed me to go to Aspen for the whole summer by myself. I lived in an old run-down hotel called the Blue Spruce. It was designed like a traditional motel, with four rooms on the bottom and an outside stairway to the four rooms on the top. A Frenchwoman named Madame Knapp was the house mistress. Madame Knapp was quite a character—rail thin, with big blonde hair, bright red lipstick, and a low, gravelly smoker's voice. She chain-smoked, and a cloud of smoke always lingered in the air above her head. The house was so old and rickety we worried that the whole place would go up in flames. We were on our own a lot and responsible for getting our meals at the cafeteria. Suddenly I was part of a group of kids more my own age, and that changed my experience for the better. I lived at the Blue Spruce every summer from then on.

At the Blue Spruce I befriended Hope Easton, a cellist from Cleveland who was even younger than me. She was tiny, with a beautiful cherubic face and the strongest little hands I'd ever seen. She had the same passion for the cello that I had for the violin. Hope later became a cellist of great renown, performing at Carnegie Hall, Lincoln Center, and venues all over the world, as well as on TV.

Hope and I became very close, even sharing a room. There wasn't a lot of space for us to practice, but we'd take turns—one of us would use the bedroom and the other would practice in the bathroom. We inspired each other to practice instead of goofing off, but we also managed to have fun together. We both had two ear piercings in our right ears, and somehow Hope talked me into letting her pierce my ear with a third hole, after freezing it with ice cubes. It was a mess—probably the grossest thing I've ever done. I still have the third hole in my ear, although it has been three decades since I've put an earring in it.

If there was any tension in our relationship it wasn't around performing, it was around boys. Our mutual crush was Peter, a cellist who also became quite renowned. That summer he was just the hottest boy at the festival. Since he was a few years older than me, I thought he was way too old for Hope. But we both went after him.

There were lots of teenagers at the festival that year. Some nights Hope and I snuck out of the Blue Spruce, which was a daring escapade. We had to climb out the window, teeter along a ledge as narrow as a balance beam, jump down, and crawl past Madame Knapp's ground-floor window. Then we headed for the hot tub at Benny Kim's place. Benny and his brother Eric were both at the music festival. Benny played the violin and Eric played the cello. They lived at a hotel with their mother. I remember skinny dipping in their hot tub late at night. We were definitely breaking curfew and might have been thrown out if we'd been caught. Luckily we never were. I became great lifelong friends with Benny, and he played my favorite violin pieces at my wedding.

Sometimes we went over to the arcade and played Pac-Man for hours. I excelled at Pac-Man, thanks to my fast, nimble hands and fierce concentration. You might say being a violinist made me a video game master. I also loved the game Galaga. I still love video games, and I was thrilled when my husband gave me Galaga and Pac-Man for Christmas recently.

The older students were a constant source of admiration. Nadja Salerno-Sonnenberg, the Italian-born classical violinist, was already a famous soloist by the time I met her, and I was in awe of her. She was five years older than me, and she played like a dream, and chain-smoked too. She was utterly cool, with tight jeans and boots, and she acted as if she didn't give a crap what anybody thought. She had attitude, and I admired that. She was the first person I'd ever seen who was a serious classical musician but looked like a rock star. Nadja went on to have a great career, although it was almost cut short by a terrible accident when she cut off the tip of one finger in a kitchen accident (thus my mom's dictate: no knives!). Her finger was reattached and her career was not damaged.

Not long ago, I was on a plane to Arizona and I realized that

Nadja was sitting behind me. Would she even remember me? I went up to her, bent down in the aisle, and said tentatively, "Nadja, I'm Gretchen Carlson. I used to go to Aspen . . ." I felt a little nervous, wondering if she would even know who I was. But she did. "Gretchen, I know who you are—how are you?" And we had a nice conversation. I glowed. Isn't it funny how you can be transported back to a teenage mentality in your forties?

Sometimes Hope, Peter Winograd, Ellen Payne, and I went into town at night to play in a quartet for money at the Souper restaurant. We were given a wonderful meal for free, and we kept a violin case open in front of us for tips. We usually made between a hundred and two hundred dollars and divided it up. Every once in a while, a celebrity would come by and drop a hundred-dollar bill into our case. My cut was a lot of money for a fifteen-year-old.

Finally I was having fun at Aspen. I belonged in a way I relished. But the main work was very serious. By this time I was in the Festival Orchestra, which was the top-ranked orchestra, and I was being personally taught by Dorothy DeLay.

Working with Dorothy DeLay was considered to be the fulfillment of any young violinist's dreams. I was in awe of her, just like every other student, but I also found her intimidating. I never felt as if we had a relationship, the way Mary and I did. I always called her "Miss DeLay," never "Dorothy." Having said that, she was a remarkable and innovative teacher. In particular she taught me to be myself, to bring forth my own voice in music. She believed that the secret to greatness was to infuse your music with your unique personality. I had never heard anyone say that before, but it was something I had already felt internally. Miss DeLay taught me a visualization technique that helped me in my life even outside violin. She asked me to visualize myself on the stage performing and to imagine the entire performance at its best, including the moment of applause or, if it was a competition, winning. She urged me to imagine the feelings. And then she'd ask me to walk it backward and visualize what I was going to do to reach that point. It was a powerful exercise, because if you can see yourself achieving the best, you have the confidence to go ahead and do it.

Miss DeLay also used visualization to help me interpret pieces. She taught me to see a piece of music as a story arc with different moods, but it would not be just any story. It would be *my* story. The personal feeling would help build the interpretation and make the piece something of my own creation.

For Dorothy DeLay playing music was not just about technique, it was about communicating. What were you trying to convey to an audience? What story were you telling? What did you want them to feel? To accomplish that you had to reach down deep inside yourself and discover the meaning of what you were playing. It was a revelation to me to begin understanding music in that way.

With Miss DeLay's guidance, I began to think in musical notes. Because I had perfect pitch, I heard them everywhere. That never went away. My husband likes to tell the story of when we lived in Cleveland right after we were married. I'd wake up in the morning and lie in the dark listening to the ships from Lake Erie blow their horns. I'd say, "E-flat . . . D-flat."

If there was a downside to working with Miss DeLay, it was that she was chronically late. She was notorious for it. Everyone joked about it, but I really hated it. I'd have a lesson scheduled for ten, and maybe if I were lucky she'd get to me by four. She was always rescheduling. I spent more time with her secretary, Leslie, than I did with her. I was a stickler for being on time, and it drove me crazy.

I guess I'd have to say she was something of a diva, and in fairness that happens when you're the best in the world and everyone wants to be with you. When I did get in to see her, the sessions sometimes felt rushed because she had twenty other students waiting. I was always conscious that I was in the presence of a great teacher who was solely focused on my craft and much less so on me as an individual. She was teaching the best players in the world, and I was only one among many. I never felt as if she paid attention to me as a person. There were no tuna sandwiches in Dorothy DeLay's studio.

By the time I was fifteen, I had a window into what my future could be. All the young players lived for their music. Some of them were just embarking on their professional careers. They were single-minded—and often unhappy. The pain and struggle of their isolated lives really struck me. I was breaking away in my own mind. I had many things I wanted to live for, not just music. Sometimes I felt guilty that I wasn't more single-minded, that I felt the strong pull of friends and school and dating and the full experience of being a young girl. During the school year, walking home from school carrying my violin, I sometimes felt embarrassed. It set me apart during a time when I only wanted to belong.

At the same time, I had an undeniable quest to persevere and excel. I believed in pushing myself beyond my limits, no matter what. Being a perfectionist was intrinsic to my personality. It was also a requirement of performing and competing. If you wanted to win, you had to be perfect. No flaws. I didn't question it then. Later in life, when I gained perspective, I saw that being a perfectionist was not such a good thing. Sometimes I thought of it as my demon. I didn't want to raise my children to think they had to be perfect, and it worried me when I saw signs that my daughter seemed to be wired that way. If she colored outside the lines, she'd throw the paper away and start over. If she got 97 instead of 100 on a test, she'd lie on the couch sobbing. I've spent a lot of time trying to make sure she understands that she doesn't have to be perfect. The drive may be intrinsic, but I'm aware that I can make it better or worse, depending on the messages I send. It's a delicate balance for parents to encourage their children to be the best they can be without burdening them with expectations that crush their individuality and creativity.

When I was younger I had dreamed of being a great soloist—traveling the world to play with orchestras everywhere, just like Itzhak Perlman, who had been one of Miss DeLay's prize pupils. There had been a time when I would have done anything to get there. In those days it was rare for women to be soloists, and that had always been my ambition. But something was happening inside me. I began to question whether being a soloist was any longer my dream.

In one respect my angst was the normal teenage desire to break free. Unfortunately, in my case breaking free had adult-sized consequences. If only I could separate my love of playing from the demands of a future career! But the two were one and the same, because success in the future demanded so much of me as a young girl. I was told repeatedly at Aspen that if I let up even a little, I might be left behind. The internal conflict was agonizing, but I wanted so much to be myself, to find myself wholly, so even as music filled my life, I tried to carve out places where I could just be me.

During the school year I did everything I could to get involved in non-violin activities. In tenth grade Molly and I both auditioned for the high school performance of *Oklahoma!* Molly got picked for the chorus, but I was not picked at all. My mom critiqued the audition and told me bluntly I didn't get a part because I was too fat and "jiggly."

I was getting tired of being considered fat. For a long time I had used my weight as a way of masking my accomplishments. I didn't want to be known as Little Miss Perfect. As long as I stayed chubby, people wouldn't hate me that much, because I had a flaw. That defense was starting to get old. There were several moments of insight—or, I should say, humiliation. One came the first time I was trying on bras. I was conscious of the woman in the dressing room poking at my breasts, and then she went out and called loudly, so that everyone in the store could hear, "I need a bigger size for the chubby girl in the dressing room." I almost died of embarrassment.

But the real turning point came because of a boy. In tenth grade I was interested in a popular basketball player at school, and I was hoping he'd ask me out. Then I overheard him tell a friend, "Gretchen has a great personality, but she's too fat to date." Was I crushed? Probably. But what I remember is a sense of resolve to make a change. Starting that very day I put myself on a diet, and was as obsessed about it as I was about everything else in my life. Within three months I'd lost thirty pounds. When I tell this story, people always ask whether or not I went out with the basketball player once I'd slimmed down. I tell them with some pride that I was no longer interested. The way I saw it, now I could do the choosing. And by the way, in eleventh grade I won the role of Chava in *Fiddler on the Roof,* and in twelfth grade I had the lead as Nellie in *South Pacific.*

Weight has continued to be a challenge for me, and to this day I have to watch my weight every single day. Sometimes people don't believe me when I say I was a chubby kid and still struggle with my weight. But I do, and it pains me to see how weight is such an esteem-crushing issue for girls, even in an era when we talk so much about empowerment.

Recalling my shame as a girl, I am serious about communicating to young women the message that they don't have to be obsessed with weight. I confess that when I was so intent on losing all that weight in high school, I was dangerously close to going too far. My self-imposed diet was all about eating almost *nothing*. Balance and health did not enter into it. I ate one graham cracker for breakfast, which I nibbled tiny bite by tiny bite. I did not eat lunch at school, except for an occasional small piece of garlic toast from the lunchroom menu. So the weight dropped off.

I remember standing in choir and hearing people behind me whispering, "Oh my God. She's getting too thin." I *liked* hearing that. I liked that people thought I was too thin in my skinny jeans. At one point my mom even expressed concern that I was losing too much weight. It was a slippery slope.

I'm grateful I didn't develop an eating disorder, but I might have. Looking back and remembering my feelings, I can see how easy it is for young girls to become dangerously obsessed with their weight. I think what saved me was that early on I had developed self-esteem from the inside instead of relying on my appearance. It's a lesson I believe in and pass on to young girls and young women whenever I have the chance. Building self-esteem from the inside is even more important today with the emphasis on being thin that pervades Hollywood and the media. That pressure makes its way into our schools and communities, where girls as young as six complain about their weight and worry about being fat. How can we expect them to feel good about themselves when we present impossible ideals? It's a no-win situation. Remember, one of the judges at the Miss America Pageant referred to me throughout his entire book as "Miss Piggy." I was 108 pounds. Today, around my kids, I am very conscious of how sensitive the issue can be, so I never talk about my weight or being on a diet. At dinner I don't have a "clean your plate" rule. Instead, I focus on delivering a message about how important it is to eat healthfully to build a strong body and mind.

For me, there's ultimately only one way to combat the struggle with body image: to know in your heart that your body does not define you. I've lived with that belief through all my own body changes. Plump or thin, I always pursued my goals with single-minded resolve. And while I worked hard to lose weight at various times in my life, I always did it for *me*, not for others.

The summer I was sixteen was a major turning point. Every summer there were two large concerto competitions for Miss DeLay's students. Participation was optional, but it was expected. If you won one of Miss DeLay's competitions it was a very big deal. You were practically guaranteed a solo career. I'd hung back for years, but I finally decided I was ready to enter.

We were each given a predetermined piece to play, and mine was Mozart's Concerto no. 5 in A major. It wasn't a particularly hard piece, but it wasn't my style. I preferred Romantic pieces, like Brahms and Tchaikovsky, pieces that allowed more room for interpretation—where I didn't feel boxed in and I could pour my heart into it.

My practice sessions with the pianist didn't go well, and for the first time I felt insecure about my performance. As the competition grew closer, I worked feverishly, but it just wasn't clicking. I didn't want to disappoint my family, who were all coming to the competition. I didn't want to disappoint Miss DeLay. And I didn't want to disappoint myself. I was always very competitive and I played to win, but I found myself dreading a competition.

I was also going through an emotional time personally, because my beloved grandma Hyllengren had recently died of cancer. She had always been there for me, attending every performance, standing up for me and letting me pour out my feelings. And now she wouldn't be around to see what I would become. It broke my heart. The whole family suffered from her loss, Grandpa most of all. Her absence made it more clear how essential her quiet, steady presence had been. The church commissioned a beautiful stained glass window dedicated to Grandma, in the front of the sanctuary by the altar. I'd sit in church and gaze at the window, talking to her in my mind. I always felt at peace when I looked at that window, just the way I felt when I was around my grandma.

But my uneasy feeling about the competition was confirmed the night of the show. I didn't even place in the top three, and the experience had a sobering effect on me. It wasn't so much that I was upset about failing. It was more the understanding—and the fear—that if I were going to step up to the next level I would have to set aside everything else in my life I enjoyed and concentrate solely on my craft. Was I willing to do that?

My parents were concerned about it and they thought maybe I'd outgrown Mary West. They told her that I would be changing teachers and signed me up to study with Lea Foli, who was the concertmaster with the Minnesota Orchestra and an elite teacher. I had my driver's license by that time, so I went alone to lessons at the University of Minnesota campus. I missed Mary, and I didn't click with Foli, although he was a great teacher. The problem was me, not him. During the time I was with Foli, I became increasingly disenchanted with the restrictions that music placed on my life. Part of it was that I had lost Mary, and in a sense I had also lost my mother, because she no longer was a constant supervisor. But that wasn't the real reason. The real reason was that I wanted more in life than music.

And that summer at Aspen what I wanted most was a certain boy. He was older than me by several years, and I was thrilled when he said he wanted to date me.

I don't know how Miss DeLay caught wind of it, but her eyes were everywhere. I remember one occasion shortly after we had started dating. It was a Sunday afternoon and I was on the stage in the big tent with Ellen Payne, playing Vivaldi's *Four Seasons,* which was written for two solo violins. Miss DeLay was sitting in the chair at the top of the tent near the entrance where she always sat during performances. And sitting right next to her was my new boyfriend. I noticed her speaking to him, but only found out later what she said: "You have a relationship with Gretchen." When he admitted it, Miss DeLay said, "Do you understand that she's jailbait?"

She seriously disapproved, and she was very protective of her underage students. She needn't have worried. Our relationship never got to the jailbait stage.

But I was smitten. When the summer ended I made up a lie to my parents about needing to stay at Aspen longer than nine weeks, but the real reason was that I wanted to hang out with my boyfriend.

The very first day the phone rang in his room. He handed it to me. "It's your mother," he said flatly.

Oh, no. Busted!

My mother's furious voice yelled over the phone, "I don't know where you are or who you're with, but you're coming home today." I'd never heard her so mad. She added, "I'm not picking you up at the airport, so you can figure out how to get home on your own."

I was upset about getting caught, and of course I felt guilty. How had she found out? It was rare for me to step off the straight and narrow, and I couldn't even get away with it. I tried not to be resentful, but I was chafing at my rigid, structured life. By the end of the summer of my sixteenth year, I was asking myself some big questions. Who was I really? Did I have a place outside of music? For the first time I was thinking about my identity, what I wanted, and what choices I had to make.

CHAPTER 3

Seize the Day

One of my high school English teachers, Jack Nabedrick, was an intense person, a tough grader but also something of a rebel. He was famous in our school for refusing to stand when the king and queen were presented each year at the Homecoming rally. He always made sure to sit in the front row so everyone would see that he was not standing. I suppose he didn't think the frivolous event merited his recognition.

Everyone in school was afraid of him, and I was no exception. I was worried about being in his class, concerned less with being able to handle the material than with how his grading might affect my straight-A average. If I was going to be valedictorian—and that was my goal—I couldn't make a single mistake. I had to achieve a 4.0.

In the beginning I was convinced that Mr. Nabedrick wouldn't like me, because although I was extremely studious, I was afraid he would spot my focus on grades above all else. I realize now that he *did* spot it and was determined to teach me an important lesson.

The first paper Mr. Nabedrick assigned was on Chaucer's *Canterbury Tales*. As usual, I worked very hard on the paper and made sure to cross every *t* and dot every *i*. After I turned it in, I waited nervously to see what grade I would get. I thought I deserved an A, and with any other teacher I would have expected it.

When he handed my paper back, Mr. Nabedrick didn't let on that there was anything unusual going on. But I immediately saw that there was no grade. Instead, there were two words written in a language I didn't understand. I was completely flummoxed. What was going on? Where was my grade?

After class I approached Mr. Nabedrick's desk. He was busy reading some papers. "There's no grade on this paper," I said, trying to hide how upset I was.

He glanced up. "I know," he said, and went back to his work.

I stood there frozen. "But why?" I asked.

He looked up again. "You'll have to figure it out," he said.

So I went to the library to look up the two words he'd written—*Carpe diem*. Then I went back to see him.

"It means 'seize the day,'" I said. "Where's my grade?"

He gave me a knowing look, and answered as before. "You'll have to figure it out."

By now I was pretty worried. I had to have a grade. What did he want me to do? I'm sure he knew that it was going to drive me bonkers, but he must have also trusted that I would somehow figure it out. I thought long and hard about what those words—"seize the day"—meant, and why he had written them on my paper. I finally realized that he wanted to make me think out of the box instead of just always expecting a perfect grade. He was challenging me to open myself to opportunities.

The words "seize the day" felt as if they were meant just for me in that moment. Tentatively I asked myself if this meant I should leave music and seize the chance to be something different.

I did get an A in his class—and also achieved my goal of a perfect 4.0 and being valedictorian. Mr. Nabedrick and his family became good friends of our family because his son was a top tennis player and my mom met them at tennis tournaments. Jack became my lifelong friend and is to this day. He often wrote me letters to encourage me. He was the first mentor I had who was not a member of my family or involved with music. Later, I invited Jack and his wife to the Miss Minnesota pageant in Austin. And when I won, he stood up and cheered. Wow! That's when I understood that maybe I had taught him something too—about being part of the moment and respecting accomplishments he hadn't deemed worthy before.

Jack gave me my motto in life: "Seize the day." Somehow he'd known that I needed to hear it and guessed that I would never have come up with it on my own. The words have permeated the way I live my life, and I keep the motto with me every single day in some shape or form.

Back in my junior year, though, I didn't really know how to make a change. Even though my passion for music was slipping, I was still committed to practicing and performing. My schedule on the weekends was strict. I was supposed to practice for four hours before I could do anything else. I wanted to get the practicing out of the way as early as possible, so I'd usually get up at six in the morning and go down to the basement. I wasn't always motivated. One day I hit upon what I thought was a brilliant idea. I had an old cassette player, and I taped myself playing. If I didn't want to practice, I'd turn on the tape and just relax, knowing the sound was wafting upstairs. I never got caught at that deception.

On the weekends I was only allowed to go out one night— Friday or Saturday. During the football season, I chose to go out Fridays so I could attend the Anoka High School football games. Molly and I would go together. We had a good time, and I was a very sociable person. But sitting home Saturday nights was hard. I became an expert on *The Love Boat* and *Fantasy Island,* which aired on Saturdays. My fantasy was to be out having fun! Still, I understood the restriction. My parents believed they were doing what was right for me. If I wanted to be the best I had to make sacrifices. And I never really missed out on anything. Being home on Saturday nights just made me appreciate it more when I did go out. And I wouldn't change any of it now! I was always telling my parents that I just wanted to be normal. But the truth was I appreciated the benefits of being unique and exceptional.

I adored my mother, but I had become quite strategic and inventive in dealing with her. I was always trying to figure out how to get around her discipline. Looking back now, I see that I was just being a normal kid, pushing the limits. Psychologists even say that it's unhealthy when kids don't rebel at all in their teenage years, because that's when they're finding out who they are as individuals. In that respect I engaged in some pretty normal teenage exploits, but at least I learned my lesson. To this day I've never touched beer, after one disastrous evening. I drank two beers and threw up all over the outside of a friend's new car. Somehow I ended up at Molly's house, which was a good thing. We called my mom and invented a story about my wanting to sleep over and I was sick long into the night. Molly had a waterbed, which didn't help my upset stomach.

In my house, whenever there was an important discussion, it took place in my parents' bedroom. There were always butterflies in my stomach as I walked up the stairs, because usually those discussions meant I was in trouble for one thing or another. In my junior year of high school we had several of these closed-door meetings. We were having "the conversation." I wanted to spend less time with music and explore other possibilities. My parents were adamant that I shouldn't stop playing the violin—that it would be tossing aside the life endeavor that had defined me since I was six. It was, they argued, my *calling.*

But was it? I could only rely on my feelings. I had no idea what the future would bring. But I wanted a chance to find out if I might have a different calling. My parents were very clear that they weren't trying to *make* me choose music as my career. They were very respectful of me. I understand that they just wanted to protect my musical promise, and also to spare me from making a rash decision that would affect the rest of my life. My mother later admitted that to some extent she was thinking of herself and the opportunities she had let pass her by when she was young. "I was smart, but I never applied myself," she told me. "I could have been a doctor. I could have been anything, but I just didn't see it then. I wanted you to appreciate your incredible gift and make the most of it so you wouldn't look back with regret."

Quitting was anathema in my family. Our motto was, "Never give up." My parents would often tell us, "We don't quit in this family." Now my mother said urgently, "Don't give up."

"I'm not giving up," I replied.

But in a sense I was. It had been percolating in me for a while, this awakening. Why would I quit something I was so good at—the music that had been the centerpiece of my life? There was no question that I could have had a career, perhaps a great one. Years later, after I won Miss America, Mary West told a newspaper reporter that I could have been one of the greatest female violinists of all time. But as a teenager, it felt like a tunnel to me, a direction in life that would shut out everything else. Besides, at that point I didn't think of it as stopping violin, just setting it aside for a time.

My parents were deeply disappointed, and I think my mother thought it might be a phase. For her it was a matter of not short-changing your God-given talents—and also always having something to be passionate about. She said, "Promise you'll find another goal to achieve—maybe one where you can use your violin talent." But she was also very cleverly thinking of more creative ways I could use my violin talent than just competing and going to Aspen.

I'm pretty sure that's how the Miss T.E.E.N. pageant came about. I was definitely not a pageant person, and I never watched pageants on TV. But my mom showed me some literature about how it was *definitely* not a beauty contest. T.E.E.N. stood for Teens Encouraging Excellence Nationally. The judging was based on grade point average, talent, interview, volunteer service, and poise. No swimsuit!

Miss T.E.E.N. was a scholarship pageant, so it had that appeal.

But for my mother there was another benefit—a chance to get me back to practicing violin and to showcasing my talent on the stage. Since I wouldn't be going to Aspen that summer, she wanted me to have a goal that included music.

I decided that since I was in it, I was going to try to win it. My competitive spirit kicked in. The competition was in late July, and I spent the spring and early summer between my junior and senior year getting ready. That meant practicing the violin, but it also meant community service, because volunteering was a big part of the score. Fortunately, I already had a lot going on in the community service arena because it was an important value in our family. No matter how busy we were, we always volunteered. I did Meals on Wheels and I helped out a woman who had multiple sclerosis. I also did a project for March of Dimes that won an award. It was a Balloon Derby. The goal was to sell balloons for a dollar each and then release them at the Pumpkin Bowl, which was the big football game on Halloween. I felt proud of that project, and to this day I am a March of Dimes volunteer as a national celebrity spokesperson and a member of the national board of trustees.

A couple weeks before the Miss T.E.E.N. pageant, I had a huge scare that shook me to the core. Anoka is considered a tornado alley. Our high school football team was the Anoka Tornadoes, and we had the Tornado marching band. I'd never experienced one in my life, but my father had talked about two very close calls when he was a child. In one instance, he was driving with his father and brother, and his father slammed on the brakes, pulled the kids out of the car, and ran down into a ditch by the side of the road. Then he lay down on top of them, shielding them with his body. Miraculously, they were unhurt.

On July 3, 1983, my mother and brothers had gone to a tennis match in Saint Paul, and Kris and I were alone in the house with Dad. We had just come home from church. It was a very heavy, humid day, and I looked out over the river and there was a green haze.

Kris and I were sitting at the kitchen table when my ears started hurting. There was terrible pressure. (My ears were always extremely sensitive to climatic changes.) I went upstairs to tell Dad, and he was standing at the big picture window looking out. The wind had started to kick up, and Dad was staring at the pontoon and the speedboat.

"My ears are killing me," I cried.

"It's okay," he said, and then his next breath was a shout: "Run!" I turned and raced down the stairs, hearing that noise people always talk about, like a train coming through.

Dad grabbed Kris and closed the back door, which was whipping in the wind. We headed for the tornado room under the stairs going down to the basement, and the three of us huddled there. It was over almost instantly—literally seconds. We stayed crouched in the tornado room for about ten minutes. Dad told us to wait and he went to take a look.

When he returned, there were tears running down his cheeks. "There is a lot of damage to the house," he said.

We staggered back upstairs. Twenty-eight trees were down on our property. The pontoon, which was a very large boat, had flown up over the high bank and landed in the neighbor's garden, mere feet from their house. Our windows were blown out. In my room I found a piece of roofing from a house across the river. It was the scariest experience of my life. And Mom and my brothers missed the whole thing.

We relocated for a few days, and I got myself together to keep preparing for the pageant. It was my secret, and the weekend I snuck off to compete, I didn't even tell my friends. It's funny now that I thought I could keep it from them. What if I won? I kept it a secret because I wasn't a "pageant person"—or at least I didn't want anyone to think I was. I knew it wasn't a beauty pageant, but I'm pretty sure that's what everybody thought.

I wore my prom dress, played the violin, and I did win. To my great humiliation, on the first day of school after the summer, the principal came on over the loudspeaker: "Big congratulations go out to Gretchen Carlson, our new Miss Minnesota T.E.E.N.!" Everyone stared at me gaping—*Whatttt?* I blushed furiously.

The national competition was scheduled for Albuquerque in December. Now I was in full competitive mode. I thought I had a good chance of winning the national title, mostly because people kept telling me I did. When I got down to Albuquerque, I heard from many people that I was certain to win—and I believed them.

When I came in first runner-up, I admit I was devastated.

One of the judges approached my parents and me after the competition. Not noticing how shattered I was, he said he was disappointed I didn't win. He told me I should try and turn the loss into something positive, and it was good advice. I didn't really hear him right away. I went up to the hotel room and cried my eyes out. I *so* didn't like to lose. As my dad always described my behavior that night, "She got her nose bent out of shape." It was true. Later, I thought about what the judge had said and wondered how I could think of my loss in a positive way.

It wasn't the first time I had to seriously consider how to make something out of failure. I'd lost competitions before, and I knew about losing. Maybe this one hit me especially hard because I had taken a risk outside my comfort zone and it hadn't paid off. Would my failure make me less inclined to take risks in the future? I was determined not to let that happen. My grandfather used to tell me that you need failure in your life to succeed, and I'd never really understood what he meant. But now I was starting to. I decided right then that I was going to keep pushing myself out of that box, keep taking risks. If I failed, I'd pick myself up and work harder.

Even with losing the competition, my senior year of high school was pretty great. I was blossoming. That's when I started dating Kurt Larson, who I would continue to date on and off for the next six years. Kurt was three years older. He was drop-dead gorgeous, but what I really appreciated was his personality. He was easygoing, incredibly nice, and very fun to be with. He represented relaxation for me. I sometimes wished I could be more like him and just roll with the punches. Most amazing, Kurt put up with all the restrictions on my time. He was so good-natured about it. And he was supportive during those times when I was stressed out.

Molly was dating Kurt's best friend, and we all went to the senior prom together. When we rode down the escalator with these two "older men," the principal and teachers who were chaperoning were alarmed. I heard one of them say, "Uh-oh." We all got a kick out of that.

I was still searching for a place in the world that would allow me to stretch my abilities beyond music. And that search aligned with making a decision about college. I never thought seriously about going to Juilliard, but other schools had strong music programs. I had earned a scholarship to the San Francisco Conservatory of Music, so that was a possibility. Mostly I was drawn to a top-of-the-line liberal arts college, where I could stretch my brain, not my violin fingers. In particular, I was interested in Stanford and

Yale. I figured I could still play, and then if I decided to pursue music later it would be an option.

My parents were pushing Yale because it was close to New York City and Juilliard, and they thought it might inspire me to keep my music interests alive. But when I visited New Haven, Connecticut, I wasn't impressed. It was raining, and the kids who took me on a tour said all they did was study. On the other hand, Stanford in Northern California was warm and sunny, with kids walking around in shorts even though it was February. That's where I wanted to go.

I agonized over the decision, and I knew the direction my parents were pushing me in. I remember we all put our choices in envelopes. I opened theirs. Yale. Yale. I opened mine. Stanford.

My heart sank at the realization of how much they wanted me to go to Yale—and how much I wanted to go to Stanford.

In the spring of my senior year, I finally chose Stanford. I almost missed the acceptance deadline—we even had to call the postmaster to come in and stamp the envelope after hours.

At Stanford I didn't have to select a major until I was a junior, but I thought about it constantly. The whole world was suddenly open to me. What would I be? I was interested in so many things. I changed my major in my mind a million times. I thought about communications, but Stanford didn't have a top program. I thought about pre-med—Stanford called it "Human Biology," or "Hum-Bio." I even thought about industrial engineering. For a while I was thinking about business school, but after I took a class in accounting I was surprised at how much I hated it. I knew one thing: I wanted to express my personality in whatever I did.

Eventually, a friend suggested majoring in organizational

behavior, and that intrigued me. It was a hot topic in the 1980s, and it would set me up to be a business consultant. I was attracted to the idea of being a problem solver and working with people to fix their companies. Organizational behavior was the major I eventually settled on, with a plan to go on to law school and become a corporate attorney.

But that was later. In the beginning, Stanford represented only one thing for me—escape. While other freshmen were embarking on the greatest challenge of their lives, I viewed college as a way to get away from the burdens imposed by my talent.

Stanford was freedom. Nobody knew who I was or that I played the violin. I was doing everything in my power to be anonymous.

I had promised my parents I'd continue studying music, but it was a promise I didn't keep. Two weeks after I arrived, I auditioned for a teacher at the music school, playing the last page of *Introduction and Rondo Capriccioso,* by Camille Saint-Saëns. When I finished, I looked up to find him staring at me dumbfounded. "Why have I not heard of you?" he finally asked. I shrugged, not answering. He couldn't have known how much I didn't want to be there. "I think we can take you on!" he said enthusiastically. I did take a class halfheartedly, but after that I put my violin in a locker at the music school and there it stayed for the whole year. I didn't take lessons or play in the orchestra. It may seem strange that I could so readily set aside music, which had been my great love, but my state of mind was cloudy. It felt like pressure, not joy.

As always, I was serious about my grades, and I studied hard, but then I stumbled with academics too. It was a class called Great Works, and my teacher just didn't like me. I don't even know why, because I read every book, while some of my classmates never cracked a page. Plato, Dante, the *Iliad*—the works. There were only eight of us in a class and we sat around a big table, and no matter what I did, this teacher was very chilly toward me. I could feel her disapproval, and I wasn't imagining it. Worse still, she gave me a C for the class. I'd never had a C in my life, and I was devastated. I didn't think I deserved it, although in hindsight it's possible that I did, and I was just so used to getting perfect grades that I was blind to my own academic flaws. Whatever the truth, that C brought down my GPA for the rest of my college career. I was used to getting all As, and I worked my fool head off for them, and that C hurt me. In the coming years I killed myself to maintain a 3.7 or 3.8, but that stupid C was like a drag on perfection. I had to accept at the very beginning of my college life that 4.0 was not attainable.

I didn't appreciate it at the time, but there was a lesson buried in this experience. Life was not about perfection. Arbitrary events and people could come along and change your trajectory. I had to come to terms with the fact that life wasn't a series of perfect moves, that working hard was important, but that sometimes it didn't create the desired result. I had to figure out how to seize the day in the face of this reality.

Even with this setback, I was doing well in my studies. I had always been a good student, and during high school I'd had my music too. Now I had nothing to worry about except going to class, which caused my mother a great deal of angst. She thought I was slacking off because I wasn't performing in the orchestra or doing volunteer work or stretching myself in other ways. Dad disagreed, telling her to let me be—that just going to classes was challenging enough. I didn't say so, but Mom was right. I was used to doing so many things at once. It was unusual for me to have just one thing to focus on. That was the way I wanted it, though. The truth is, I was tired. I needed the break.

Mom didn't stop worrying, though, and she was still trying to find ways to keep my music going. She believed my talent should be showcased. So she arranged for me to do a big recital in Minnesota after my freshman summer and right before I started my sophomore year. It wasn't exactly that I was being forced to do the recital, but my parents did pull the "we're paying for college" card.

I had been looking forward to the summer of my freshman year. I'd found my first summer job outside my dad's dealership, as a waitress in an Italian restaurant at the mall. It was a lousy job, but I got it on my own. But my parents made me quit after three weeks to practice for the recital.

Putting together a whole recital was very challenging. It was something all great young artists did as a way of coming into their own. I thought I put together a pretty impressive program, even though my heart wasn't 100 percent in it. I did nothing but practice that summer, and I barely saw Kurt. I was relieved when the day of the recital came and went. But I overheard the man running the audio say he didn't think I'd performed that well. Who was he to judge? His stinging remark really hurt.

My mother kept strategizing about ways to put musical opportunities in front of me, and that's how the idea of the Miss America pageant came up at the end of my junior year. I'd been happy at Stanford, and I was excelling. I was lucky enough to spend the spring quarter at Oxford, and before I left for England I learned that I'd also been accepted to an international business course through Georgetown University that would allow me to stay at Oxford for the summer.

Oxford was for me the quintessential learning experience. My classes were so different than Stanford's. They weren't lectures, they were tutorials where you got to work one-on-one with a professor. You could choose your topic, and I decided to take on a challenge and study twentieth-century women's literature, a subject I knew nothing about.

For my first class I went to the professor's house and we sat in her tiny study and read Virginia Woolf and discussed her novels. I was intimidated at first, because the spotlight was completely on me and my ability to make sense of the material. But it was also exciting and felt like a very adult learning experience.

The workload was demanding, and I didn't have a lot of free time. There was a pub down the street from our dorm, and they stopped serving drinks at 11:00 p.m. So we'd study like crazy until about 10:00 and then make a mad dash down to the White Horse Pub. I don't drink beer, so I'd order alcoholic cider, called scrumpy cider. As it got close to 11:00, we'd order extra drinks and sit there talking and drinking.

May Day was a big celebratory event in England. We drank Pimm's liqueur mixed with ginger ale, and it was awful, but we didn't care. We stayed up all night, dancing in the streets and watching the crew races and eating scones with jelly and whipped cream.

At Oxford I learned to drink my tea with sugar and cream—and to eat. It was like heaven for me because we were eating all the time. Tea with crumpets in the morning, tea with sandwiches in the afternoon. And that was in addition to lunch. The pub food was heavily fried, and I tried valiantly to find healthy things to eat. But I wasn't very successful. Of course I gained weight.

Then one day late in the quarter my mother called me. "You have to come home for the summer," she said. "I've found the perfect pageant for you."

"What are you talking about?" I grumbled. "I'm registered for the Georgetown program."

"Hear me out," she insisted. "I'm reading about the new director of the Miss America pageant. His name is Leonard Horn. He says they're changing the direction this year, putting more focus on excellence and less focus on the beauty element, because this is, after all, a *scholarship* pageant. Here, let me read it to you: 'Miss America is a relevant, socially responsible achiever whose message to women all over the world is that in American society a woman can do or be anything she wants.' Leonard Horn says he wants Ivy League contestants, people who have honed their talents for their whole lives."

She paused, and then said firmly into the phone, "That's *you*, Gretchen."

Mom and I had talked about the Miss America pageant before—she was convinced I could nail the talent portion, which was a big part of the score. But so much else was going on in my life, and the idea had faded to the background. Now, listening to Mom, I felt the familiar tingle of the competitive drive. If I did the pageant, it would be the most challenging goal I had ever pursued, because even though I had achieved great things in my youth, the Miss America pageant was outside my comfort zone. It would mean starting as an underdog and stretching myself in new ways.

"Because of Leonard Horn, this is the year where the focus on talent and academic achievement will be the greatest," Mom said. "I think this is your year."

And so I decided to seize the day.

CHAPTER 4

Becoming Miss America

When most people think of the Miss America pageant, they envision a night of pomp and glitter on a big stage in Atlantic City, where in a dazzling finale one young woman is crowned. In reality, Miss America is a long journey that begins in hundreds of small towns across the country, with ordinary girls just like me. It's not an event, but a competitive process, similar to qualifying for the Olympics, where winning at various levels advances you to the next.

The first step is winning the pageant from a local community to become eligible for the state pageant. Some states require that you live in the community; others allow anyone from across the state to enter open pageants. There weren't a lot of open pageants in my area, but I found one in Cottage Grove, a suburb of Saint

Paul, and I entered that one. Winning would qualify me for the Miss Minnesota pageant, and winning Miss Minnesota would qualify me for the Miss America pageant.

I came home from London in June 1987, and the Miss Cottage Grove contest was in August. I had little time to prepare, and I needed to do a lot of work.

I immediately found a coach in Kathleen Munson, who ran the Pageant Shop in the Twin Cities. Kathleen was very tall, with short red hair and an infectious personality, cheering me with her southern twang. She was originally from Tulsa, Oklahoma, and the pageant was in her blood. Kathleen cautioned me that I was in for a long haul—a victory that might be years in the making. In the South, she said, they put girls on a "four-year plan" to be contestants. "You shouldn't expect to win the pageant the first year you try it," she cautioned. I didn't argue the point, but I wasn't intending to make this a multiyear project. I was in it because I wanted to win it—that year.

Kathleen had an office set up in the basement of her house, where she put me through my paces, introducing me to a foreign world. Until then I had never given a single moment's thought to the way I walked. Now I felt as if I were learning an elaborate dance. "The walk," as I called it, was one of my biggest fears. I had always been a tomboy, not a model. Kathleen made me practice in high heels, and I'd totter along the twenty-foot runway she'd set up, feeling enormously clumsy.

Kathleen showed me pictures of pageant winners she had groomed, and they all seemed to have perfect dresses, perfect bodies, and flawless hair and makeup. It was the first time in my life I was awed by something girly. I had never played "princess" as a child. The glamour side of the pageant was totally foreign to me. At the same time, the talent side was somewhat foreign to Kathleen, and when she heard me play the violin she was a bit taken aback. I think it made her look at me with new respect.

Working with Kathleen was more than just a lesson in the mechanics of a pageant. It was also about the *psychology* of a pageant. She always said that you can't teach charisma or authenticity, and the key was to let your personality shine through. She stressed that personality was the main attribute of a winner.

I believed that. One of the big complaints about Miss America pageants in the 1980s was that everyone felt so canned—overcoached and overdressed. That wasn't my style, and normally that might have been a disadvantage. But that year I thought it was my strength.

Kathleen's sessions were like a crash course in pageantry and its strategies. I realized that many of my competitors would have much more experience than I, especially if they'd been on the so-called four-year plan. That turned out to be the case. A lot of the contestants had been in the system for a while. The states had different rules for how many times a person could compete, but it wasn't unusual for people to try again if they didn't win the state title the first time. But for me the goal was to compete, succeed, and then go on with my studies and my life.

Mom and I mapped out a strategy for how I might win. In general, my theory of competing was to do it through observation, not participation. I was going to watch how others did it and learn by studying them. Part of the plan was literally *intel*. I went to the Miss Minnesota pageant, and Mom, Dad, and I planned to attend the Miss America pageant in Atlantic City to gather information.

Unfortunately, I got sick and couldn't go to Atlantic City, but my parents went anyway and brought back their valuable observations, which went right into our strategy.

My first serious task was getting in shape. I was not confident about my body. I'd just spent a semester in London, and it seems that all we did was eat. But I had less than two months before the Miss Cottage Grove pageant, so it was a matter of trying to make the most of what I had. My mom and I went shopping for a dress, and we picked a white gown off the rack. Even though it was inexpensive, Mom knew how to work magic on a dress so that it looked great.

Fortunately, the Miss Cottage Grove competition was relatively low-key. It was held in the local high school, and most of the contestants were there to have fun and maybe earn a little money for college. The winner received $1,000 in scholarship money, $500 for clothing and training, and discount coupons for local businesses. There was a homespun quality to it, and the people running it were all volunteers from the Jaycees. For me the hardest part—and this would continue to be true—was the dance number. I was not a dancer. They always put me in the back row. Our opening number was a dance to Neil Diamond's "Coming to America." All I can say about my performance is that I didn't fall down.

What I remember most was how nice and supportive everyone was. After I won Miss Cottage Grove, the organizers continued to support me as if they saw themselves as surrogate parents. Some of them continued to befriend and guide me throughout the pageant process, and I found that incredibly touching. They really cared about me. I was their girl.

After the Miss Cottage Grove contest, Mom and I visited Canton, Ohio, to check out a gown shop called Suzie Lee. That's where we bought the green-and-black talent gown that would take me all the way through Miss America. It cost $250. While we were there, we attended the Miss Canton pageant, which was much larger than Miss Cottage Grove. We were serious about collecting information wherever we could.

In October I returned to Stanford, but any thought that I might be able to juggle college and pageant preparation was quickly dashed. I realized that if I was going to continue to pursue Miss America I would have to put my studies on hold until after the pageant.

In December I went to the dean to tell her I was "stopping out"—meaning taking a leave from my studies. I wasn't planning to explain why, but when she asked I sheepishly replied, "To try and become Miss America."

"That's absolutely the most ridiculous thing I've ever heard," she said bluntly. I think she wondered incorrectly why someone who had made it into Stanford with incredibly good grades would want to become Miss America. I didn't bother trying to explain that Miss America was mostly about talent, scholarship, and presence—that I'd been a concert violinist in childhood and talent was half the points. I just walked away and started packing my stuff.

I told very few people about my reasons for leaving, and later, when I became Miss America, many of my professors and fellow students told the media how shocked they were. They'd had no idea. I'd just disappeared.

I didn't even tell my sorority sisters. Part of the reason was that I didn't want to set myself up in case I failed. Another part was that I just didn't want to contend with the doubters. I knew what the pageant meant to me, but I was well aware of what many other people thought, and I didn't want to deal with explaining away the old stereotypes.

The pageant became my full-time job. I had only nine months to prepare. Most of that preparation would go into competing for the title of Miss Minnesota in June. If I won, it would be less than two months until the Miss America pageant in Atlantic City. So my preparation for Miss Minnesota was really my main preparation for Miss America.

The first thing I had to do was get in shape, which meant losing fifteen to twenty pounds. I immediately started working out with Mike Tracy, a local trainer who was used to getting women in shape for pageants. He worked at the club that my family belonged to, but I was nervous about starting with him, so I did aerobics on my own for a couple of weeks so I wouldn't look like a complete schlub when he met me. When we finally got together, Mike put me on a strict diet—twelve hundred calories a day and practically no fat. I had to write down everything I ate and bring him my diet journal so he could sign it. I was always hungry. Like most people, I knew how to lose weight; it was doing it that was hard.

Working out with Mike was extremely challenging. He had me running, lifting weights, rowing—a full range of physical activities. He was like a drill sergeant. He never let up on me. And I took it because I was motivated. Mike always told people I took the most pain of anyone he'd ever trained.

The hardest part was running. I was still haunted by my teenage anxiety when I had to run in the President's Fitness Challenge, but I also found it boring and grueling. For the pageant preparation I knew I had to do it, so I just got into a mentality of mind over matter and forced myself. I used Miss DeLay's old trick of visualization, imagining positive images as I ran. I realized I was pushing myself to do something I had never done before, and my competitive drive kicked in. When I eventually got up to six miles, I could hardly believe it, but by then it was second nature.

My schedule was fierce—three or four hours a day practicing the violin, two hours of pageant coaching, two hours of working out. And in between I was studying—yes, studying. I wanted to be knowledgeable about current events and to develop a point of view about what was going on in society so I could do well in the interviews and answer questions intelligently.

It was ironic that I was back in the lonely groove of competing. All my friends were away at school, and I wouldn't have had time for them anyway. The only person around was Kurt. He was a rock. He worked out with me, and I bought a racing bike so we could race together. We were both getting into world-class shape. But my mom had put me on a strict curfew—ten o'clock. It seemed silly for a twenty-one-year-old to have a curfew, but she was determined that my focus would be solely on the competition, and she was right.

I was exercising so hard I could have eaten a farm. But of course I was on a strict diet. I'd get up in the morning and eat half a bowl of cereal and half a banana, and by ten I was ravenous. So I ate another half a banana. Visions of home cooking danced in my head. But I never wavered. It was all part of the discipline, the price I would pay to win. It was a necessity.

And then there was the violin. It had been years since I'd played seriously, and I hunkered down to prepare for the performances of my life. I was a bit rusty, but that didn't affect my confidence. I believed in myself. I knew that my talent, even at 75 percent, was still top-notch and couldn't be touched in the first few phases of a competition. I even chose a piece for the Miss Minnesota pageant that I had never played before—the *Carmen Fantasy* on themes from the passionate opera. I had six months to perfect it. Once I started practicing, I was instantly back in my old mode. I discovered that the competitive spirit never goes away. Returning to music taught me something, not just about playing the violin, but about having that fire, that desire to achieve. It's what I'd been missing in my life, and it felt right to be back into it. Along with putting aside the violin in college, I had also put aside my drive, thinking it was time for a rest. But I saw that I needed it, I was born with it. You can teach people skills to hone their craft, but unless they have the fire in their belly, the skills don't matter. I never again let my passion slide. The insatiable desire—the appetite—to always get better still drives me today.

In April, Mom and I started to deal with important decisions like wardrobe, and we stepped it up a notch, making visits to the people who were tops in the pageant field.

Our first trip was to Fort Worth to meet with Ann Bogart, who was *the* swimsuit designer for pageants. That meeting was memorable for how many pegs I got knocked down. Ann and her husband were Russian immigrants. Ann was small, but she had a very daunting manner. I think her attitude was that the best contestants were southern girls because they had the right style. The fact that I was from Minnesota was not a point in my favor when it came to the Miss America pageant. She thought midwestern girls were too "natural," and she didn't mind saying so. She studied my body, frowning.

"Have you ever done pageants before, honey?"

"Not really. I've never been in the Miss America system."

"You'll never win," she declared.

"Well, I'm giving it my best shot," I said weakly.

"What's your talent?"

"Violin."

She snorted. "Violin's never won. You're going to have to fiddle."

I almost laughed. I had been playing classical music my whole life, and that's a whole different craft than fiddling.

Finally she got down to brass tacks. "What kind of swimsuit do you want?"

"Rose-colored," I said naively.

"Rose!" she screeched in disbelief. "Oh, no, no, no. Only white wins."

So why'd she ask?

Ann and her husband, Louis, lived in a rambler, which was totally devoted to swimsuits. At the back of their kitchen was a huge area cluttered with sewing machines and fabric swatches. We looked through the swatches and settled on a coral pink. Not white. I wondered if she thought I was a hopeless case. I ended up having her make the coral suit for the Miss America pageant, but I bought a white suit off the rack to compete for Miss Minnesota.

Ann had a secret material for her swimsuit creations. It hugged your body in all the right places to enhance your bustline and slenderize your waistline. I appreciated the help. In those days we were limited to a simple one-piece. Today contestants can wear two-piece suits. Thank God I didn't have to wear a two-piece!

Had I been a less secure person, I would have walked out of Ann's home a shambles. But I'd learned my lessons about failure and perseverance, and I didn't dwell on her criticisms. Months later at the Miss America pageant she happened to be sitting in front of my parents. After I finished my violin solo, she turned around and said apologetically, "Maybe that fiddling idea wasn't such a good one after all."

Next stop was Austin, where I met with Chuck Weisbeck, who was known as the "coach of the Queen" and, alternatively, "the Butcher." His studio was famous for whipping pageant contestants into shape. As he once put it, with a devilish Texas drawl, "All I have to do is torture these girls and make 'em look good." Weisbeck was seventy, and he'd been training people for twice as long as I'd been alive. He was tall, with a craggy, aging face and a head of curly gray hair. He wore a shimmery sweat suit that squeaked when he moved. His wife, Artie, also about seventy, had a big bouffant hairdo and a ton of makeup. She didn't look like she actually did all the exercises, but she was a trained coach.

Chuck was quite a character. His studio was lined with portraits of pageant contestants in swimsuits, women he'd trained, including many winners. He was completely unrelenting in what he called the three P's of working out: "Puff, pant, and perspire." And he didn't care a whit about embarrassing me. I thought I was in pretty good shape by that point, but he grabbed my thigh and said, "This has got to go!" He stared at my butt and cried, "Absolutely not!" He declared that my body had to be rehabbed to achieve the right "cut," and he taught me his system of "plyometrics," a challenging circuit program using no equipment, designed to increase both speed and power in an explosive way. He ordered me to return home and work out every day in my basement.

While I was doing plyometrics in my basement, and still running every day, my dad would come home for lunch and hear me down there. One day he asked my mom, "Is she going to die down there from working out too hard?" He wasn't kidding.

I was told that I should aspire to create "diamonds of light" in the spaces between my legs. That's another thing I'd never considered before—the spaces between my legs. I thought of my great grandmother with her solid legs—not a hint of light to be seen. I had that inheritance to overcome. As a chubby child, I'd had no space between my thighs, but now I had to work to get that "light" at five different places. It made my head spin.

Our final mother-daughter road trip stop was Greenville, South Carolina, to meet with Stephen Yearick, the gown designer. On our way to his shop, we stopped at Burger King, where we had a difference of opinion about how much money we would spend on my custom evening gown. I thought we'd have to spend way more than my mom was budgeting. I'd heard the stories of contestants who spent big bucks and ordered several different gowns. I was looking at only one gown, but I assumed it would be pricey.

Stephen was genuine and extremely charming. Bursting with fervor, he promised me, "It will be *fabulous*! We'll put together the most *fabulous* evening gown for you!" My mother and I loved his enthusiasm. He was good, and better still, he made *me* feel good.

Stephen had a roomful of dresses for me to try on. I told him I wanted to look taller. We settled on a design, a silk dress with elaborate beading that would be done overseas. Dresses are simpler these days and you rarely see beading, but this was the 1980s and everything was ostentatious. When Stephen designed my gown, we were pleasantly surprised when he said it would be under $3,000. He might have been taking pity on me, thinking I didn't have a chance of winning, but we were thrilled with the result.

Stephen was a genius, and his process was fascinating. To customize my gown to perfection he fitted a muslin fabric over my body and pinned it exactly to every inch and curve so the dress would fit me alone. After the gown arrived from overseas we had to get creative about the bra. Since the gown was low in the back it was impossible to wear a regular bra or even a corset bra because it would have left a visible line at the waist. It needed to be perfect, and this was in the days before Spanx! So we figured out a contraption and had a seamstress make it. It was an underwire bra that went around my armpits and down around each leg with a loop to give me support but hide any chance of lines.

Let me add that I wore that gown to my twenty-fifth Miss America anniversary in September 2013—the first time I'd put it on since the pageant. A big breakfast was planned for five hundred people. I called Stephen a few days before the event. "I have a hare-brained idea to try and get into my competition gown for the anniversary," I said. There was silence on the other end of the phone. I could guess what he was thinking—that I'd be lucky to squeeze even my big toe into that dress!

"Stephen?" I said into the silent phone. "Uh, I need your help." He told me to meet him with the dress at a place in Times Square called Bra Tenders, which is a specialty undergarment shop for actresses and theater folks. I went into the dressing room with a woman who pulled a few Spanx garments out and a few bras. I tried on the dress, and, much to my shock, we could zip it up! It was a little tight, but it was on. When we opened the curtain to show Stephen, he gasped. "Oh my God!" he cried. "I can't believe you can get that on. Your boobs look fabulous!" Truth is, after two kids and more "maturity," my boobs were bigger than when I was a twenty-two-year-old skinnier version of myself.

The gown was also much shorter than when I wore it in the pageant. I figured it was because I was wearing five-inch platform heels, and back in 1988 the highest heels I could find were three inches. Stephen helpfully observed that it might also be shorter because it was tighter and it cinched up.

Four days later at the breakfast, Stephen was my partner in crime in the women's bathroom off to the side of the huge ballroom where I was going to be announced before coming out to speak. We had snuck off to the bathroom in the middle of the program so he could help me get into the gown.

Sam Haskell, the CEO of the pageant, did a wonderful introduction of me and played a video on the big screen of my talent performance and my crowning. I then walked out on the stage in my pageant dress and the whole room gasped and applauded. It was a sweet moment. My parents were seated at the front table and I honored them as my best friends and for always being my rock and foundation in life. It was a very moving event.

The Miss Minnesota pageant took place in June at the Riverside Arena in Austin, Minnesota, a rural area near Rochester, where the Mayo Clinic is. Austin is famous for Hormel ham. There were twenty-four contestants, and my number was twenty-two, which was great because that was my lucky number.

Compared to Miss Cottage Grove, the state competition was the "big time," since the winner would represent the whole state and go on to Atlantic City. Even so, there was a nice homespun quality about it. During the pageant I lived in a sponsor home with another contestant. We slept upstairs in a guest room with twin beds. Lowell and Faye Anderson were a wonderful couple, and I was touched by how warm and welcoming they were, making us feel right at home. I remember that Faith made delicious mini-muffins that we later dubbed "lucky muffins" after I won.

The four competitive events were talent, swimsuit, evening gown, and interview. We started in small groups and then advanced through to the finals. I wore the white bathing suit in the swimsuit portion, and Ann Bogart was right. I actually looked pretty good in that swimsuit. In fact, I "won" in my initial group of four, which was quite a surprise—not to mention a vindication. In the talent competition when I played the *Carmen Fantasy*, I knew I'd nailed it. The applause was deafening. I won the preliminary talent award for the whole pageant.

My question was what I saw as the greatest challenge facing the country. I said, "The breakdown of the family," pointing out that other problems were a manifestation of that. I felt pretty satisfied with my answer. I believed it, and I'm sure it went over well in Minnesota, which is a family-values state.

By the finale, I was feeling pretty confident, but you never know. At the end I was standing there with one other contestant, and when they called her name as first runner-up, I realized I had won. I beamed and cried. I'd actually done it!

So it was on to Miss America. I immediately started doing intel on the other state winners, getting tapes of their talent segments so I could see what I was up against. I studied them intently. I also watched as many tapes as I could find from former Miss America pageants.

The pageant was on September 10 and I had less than two months to prepare. Actually, I had *no* time to prepare, because I was busy traveling the state making appearances as Miss Minnesota. My mind was already in Atlantic City, and it was hard to manage everything I had to do. But I loved my state, and the people were incredibly enthusiastic. On several weekends I toured the state and stayed in the homes of wonderful families. These were mostly small towns, just like Anoka, and the people greeted me with open arms. I wished I had more opportunity to relax and enjoy the experience, but the big competition loomed ahead of me.

There was a lot of pressure, but most of it came from inside. Many years later I was amused to come across a Q&A I did for a local newspaper after I won Miss Minnesota. The answers are quite revealing:

> **Nobody would believe it if they saw me:**
> "Relaxed."

> **I can die happy once I've:**
> "Eaten over 1,200 calories every day of my life."

> **I've never been able to:**
> "Go away on vacation when I didn't have to
> worry about anything."

Some people might say that level of drive is unhealthy, but while there were times of stress, for the most part I found the process of pursuing a goal to be exhilarating and sometimes joyful. Sure, it was tempting to imagine kicking back and not having a care in the world, but that wasn't me, and I understood that about myself.

I was still preparing like crazy, especially for the interview, which was a big part of the pageant. The pageant people set up mock interviews, which my dad helped with, gathering panels of friends and businesspeople from the community. They'd throw every question they could think of at me. Sometimes it was pretty comical. I remember one panel was held in someone's basement. One of the first questions was, "What do you think of euthanasia?" I didn't know what euthanasia was—what I heard was *youth in Asia*—so I gamely replied, "I think it's great young people can travel to Asia." Answers like that can get you pegged forever as dumb, but everyone thought it was funny. To this day I get teased by some people about it.

My "euthanasia" mistake proved why practicing the interview so many times was important. Dad set up some mock interviews at his car dealership, and we videotaped them and learned a lot. For example, I saw that I always gestured with my right hand when I spoke, so I had to work on that. I also practiced sitting. Some years the interviews were held standing up, but our year we'd be seated, so I tested out different hemline lengths. Not a single detail went unnoticed.

Another important piece of the preparation was filling out the contestant fact sheet. My mom and I worked on this for weeks. The judges would use it as their reference point, and our strategy was to make it full of information that was interesting, would help me stand out, and we hoped would keep the interview focused on me personally and not so much on world events. I was well aware that the interview was the first impression the judges would have of me, and I figured the more they knew and liked me, the better my score would be. On my fact sheet I stressed my academics and my violin performances—especially performing with Isaac Stern and the Minnesota Orchestra. I also added personal details—my love of sushi, my perfect pitch, my international travels, and the fact that my grandfather was the minister of the second largest Lutheran church in America. My ambition? "To be the first Miss America with a classical violin talent; to complete my undergraduate degree at Stanford University; to enter into graduate law studies."

I felt as ready as I'd ever be, but some people still thought of me as an underdog because of my height. Even my beloved grandfather told me before the pageant that I would probably lose.

"Sparkles, you're a lovely girl, but you're never going to be Miss America," he said.

"Why not?" I tried not to sound offended.

"You're too short," he said.

I refused to take that as fact. Had there never been a short Miss America? I went to the library and found a book on the Miss America pageant. I discovered that the very first Miss America in 1921, Margaret Gorman, was five foot one. I had two and a half inches on her! I ran back to set my grandfather straight.

A week before the pageant, it turned out that I had a worse problem than my height. I started getting water blisters all over my face. I panicked. What was going on? My mom drove me to the dermatologist, who took one look at me and said, "Oh, this isn't good."

I was alarmed. "What is it?" I demanded, almost ready to cry. "I'm leaving to compete in the Miss America pageant next week and I really need it to go away."

She stared at me in disbelief. "You're going to compete in the Miss America pageant looking like *that*? You have facial warts."

Facial warts? I was too stunned to speak.

"This condition is usually related to stress," the doctor explained. "Do you have any unusual stress in your life right now?" Was she kidding? "Oh, I guess so." But not to worry. She had a prescription cream she said would clear it right up. And it did.

The experience gave me pause, though. I had spent my whole

life knowing how to manage many things at one time and always succeeding, and this was no different. Except that my body was finally telling me how much stress I was really under by supplying a very unpretty physical manifestation.

I arrived in Atlantic City, with my fifty fellow contestants, ten days before the pageant. I was assigned to my room, which I would be sharing with a traveling companion from my state. The pageant is a very well-chaperoned event. You're never alone. Each day your personal chaperone hands you off to a member of the National Hosting Committee, who is responsible for your safety and well-being, transportation, and all other necessities. All of these guides and chaperones are very well vetted, and most of them have lots of experience. They became an important emotional support system as well, since they'd been through it so many times before. They kept telling me, "Relax and enjoy the experience," and if I was able to do that at all, it was thanks to them.

The theme of the show, in keeping with the new focus on achievement, was "A Salute to Success!" Most of our time the first few days was spent practicing the lavish production numbers, which are a big part of the televised show but do absolutely nothing for you in terms of winning. The opening number was an intensely choreographed song and dance number called "Success." Luckily, they had professional dancers, dubbed "the Miss America dancers," doing a slick routine, while we paraded behind them, singing and smiling—wearing outfits that weren't that attractive but were very 1980s. Mine had black and white polka dots with outlandishly puffy shoulders. The second number was a tropical-themed routine, an homage to Kaye Lani Rae Rafko, Miss America 1988's talent number, which had been a Tahitian dance performance. Once again the Miss America dancers took the lead, along with Kaye Lani, while the rest of us, draped in leis, made Tahitian-style movements. I was way in the back, up on a platform. I had never been a sexy, flaunt-my-body dancer kind of person, or a dancer at all. I took ballet for one month when I was five, and I hated it. Of course, they picked the best dancers for the front row. Believe me, I wasn't one of them.

We also practiced every aspect of the televised pageant—how to walk out in a swimsuit and evening gown, where to twirl, where to stand, and even how to win. A mock Miss America winner was chosen to walk the runway, so we could see how it was done.

For the first time that year, Miss America had two panels of judges. The first panel judged the preliminaries and selected the top ten contestants, who would be featured in the television broadcast. The second panel of celebrity judges made the final decisions on pageant night. The celebrity judges, who would be sitting in an orchestra pit below the stage, were Eileen Ford, Eva Gabor, Deborah Norville, Brian Boitano, Phyllis George, George Peppard, Richard Dysart, Walter Anderson, Blair Underwood, Dr. Joyce Brothers, William Farley, and Lili Fini Zanuck. I was nervous about being judged by Eileen Ford. I knew this wasn't strictly a beauty pageant, but she judged models and rejected any who weren't at least five foot eight—preferably taller. I was also worried I wouldn't have a supporter in Eva Gabor (although she was five foot two), but I was dead wrong. Eva loved me. Later, when I was on the road in California, she took me shopping on Rodeo Drive in her fancy car. She said she wanted to do it because, she said, "People tell me you look like my daughter." Very sweet.

Once the judges were announced, I studied their backgrounds to try and get to know them. Where possible I found out their opinions on important issues so I wouldn't inadvertently offend them. (It never occurred to me until William Goldman wrote about it that talking about my values and faith would be offensive to anyone.)

I did wonder how the celebrity judges could really understand the contestants and the contest enough to make the right decisions. I found out in 2000 when I was a celebrity judge. You're schooled thoroughly on the pageant, the process, and the top ten contestants. You spend a considerable amount of time getting to know who these women are—not just on the stage, but their backgrounds, achievements, and aspirations. It made me feel better about the celebrity judges many years earlier.

The preliminary judges were responsible for four days of mini-pageants, Tuesday through Friday. Tuesday was swimsuit, Wednesday talent, and Thursday evening gown. On Friday we had the Miss America Boardwalk Parade. Interviews were held on Tuesday.

The preliminary point system was:

> Talent: 50 percent
> Swimsuit: 15 percent
> Evening gown/personality/expression: 15 percent
> Interview: 20 percent

On Saturday night the final point system for the top ten contestants would be:

> Talent: 40 percent
> Swimsuit: 20 percent
> Evening gown/personality/expression: 40 percent

The interview on Tuesday was seven minutes long, and I remember entering the room feeling nervous but ready to take on the challenge. I had studied hard to prepare for any question that might get asked, but this wasn't a current events quiz. I was well aware that the celebrity judges would also be reviewing the interview, and it would be a factor in their decision. I left the room hoping I had made a good impression. You only have one shot at a first impression. Years later when I read William Goldman's book I saw what he thought of me: "Real bright, chunky, self-possessed." He said I would have made the "most dedicated Sunday school teacher in the history of the world." I know he meant it as a jab, because I stressed the importance of values. I don't think of it as an insult one bit. He also wrote that I had more chance of winning than *he* did. But not much.

A year after my pageant, Miss America formally introduced the concept of a platform, which required each contestant to choose an issue about which she cared deeply and that was of relevance to our country. During her year as Miss America, she would use the title to further her platform. It was a wonderful addition, but in my year we didn't have the platform yet. If there had been one, mine would have been my life's passion—the fine arts and education—which I ended up stressing during my entire year on the road. My interview questions stayed pretty close to the fact sheet that my mom and I had spent countless hours perfecting. That strategy proved to be a good one, as it kept the judges focused more on what I'd done in my life and less on controversial issues.

In the preliminary we went through all the paces, and the judges had to watch everyone compete and rate us individually on the score sheet. Only the top ten would be competing in the televised show.

It was a crushing schedule, and a tremendous challenge. When you're in this kind of situation you're always fighting to keep your confidence levels high. I'd get up early and run on a treadmill in the mornings, trying to focus my mind. Whenever I could during the day, I slipped away to practice my violin. There were rooms upstairs in the convention center—they were up near the rafters and a little scary—and I used whatever time I could steal, even if it was only a few minutes, as solo time for my fingers and my mind. I needed it! The dance rehearsals were so demoralizing, and those breaks always restored my spirits.

In spite of my determination to stay focused, a big blow came three days before the pageant. The Atlantic City newspaper published the predictions of a retired statistics professor named George Miller, who had developed a computer program designed to pick the next Miss America. He'd correctly selected five of the last ten Miss Americas, including runners-up. Miller entered information into the program such as height, eye color, hair color, weight, measurements, and talent. His pick for my year was Miss Arkansas, followed by Miss Pennsylvania and Miss South Carolina. I didn't even make the top ten. Commenting on my talent—I was the only violinist that year—Miller said that sometimes violinists made the top ten, but they never won. Why? "It's hard to emote with that thing under your chin."

Clearly, though, Miller gave the most weight to beauty, declaring that the single most important thing you could do to win Miss America was to win the swimsuit competition. Oh, and be tall.

It frustrated me that people still thought that Miss America was about choosing the perfect physical specimen. People confused the pageant with Miss USA, which feeds into the Miss Universe pageant, and that really *was* a beauty contest. If I'd entered Miss USA, I would have been dead last. I wasn't a model, and I could never walk like one.

Yes, it was fun to put on beautiful clothes and have my makeup and hair done—albeit 1988-style hair! But that was never the main impetus for me. I was competing because I knew I could nail the talent and achievement portions. The rest was extra. Without my talent I would never have been Miss America.

Times had definitely changed. Back in the 1920s when the pageant first started, the only thing that mattered was how you looked. I mean *only*. The scoring was entirely devoted to perfection head to toe: fifteen points for construction of head, ten for eyes, five for hair, five for nose, five for mouth, ten for facial expression, ten for torso, ten for hands, ten for legs, ten for arms, and ten for grace of bearing. Whew! That list gives me pause, especially the score for construction of head. My parents always talked about how I had an odd-shaped head as a baby. I guess I would have been out of luck with that scoring method.

We were in a new era, but there were still ongoing protests that the Miss America pageant was a crass objectification of women. I had heard that there was some upset in the Miss California pageant my year when one of the contestants, Michelle Anderson, said she had entered for the sole purpose of going to Atlantic City and exposing the way the pageant demeaned women. She didn't win, but when they announced the winner, she rushed onto the stage and pulled a silk scarf out of her chest that read "Pageants Hurt All Women."

But I saw it differently. For me and for most of the contestants, winning Miss America was not about being crowned the most beautiful Barbie. I'm not saying looks didn't enter into it, although I wasn't even close to being the prettiest. It was about competing on a high level and challenging myself to be at the top of my game. It was also about winning scholarship money that would help me pursue my dreams. This wasn't the 1920s. We all had a lot going on—and by the way, I say to this day that there's nothing wrong with being smart, talented, *and* attractive.

In that respect, Miller's computer system was anachronistic. Still, it got a tremendous amount of play, although as it turned out none of the contestants he picked even made it to the top ten. I have to admit it shook my confidence. Miller quit doing predictions after my year, grumbling that "they've downgraded swimsuits so much that it took care of poor old George. They're getting better people. They seem brighter and come from better schools." In other words, attributes harder to measure with a computer program. I was glad to hear him say it, but at the time the computer results really upset me.

The preliminaries for talent, swimsuit, and evening gown were held at the convention center, and people could buy tickets to come and watch, so the seats were always full—mostly with enthusiastic fans, family members, and pageant devotees. We wouldn't find out who was in the top ten until we were on television Saturday night.

Each morning before I left the hotel, I had my makeup done, because the makeup artists weren't allowed in the hall. I had brought in a fabulous lady named LuAnn Mancini, a talented Texan whose claim to fame was that she did Dan Rather's makeup— which shows her range. LuAnn was a delight and something of a genius. She had perfected an airbrushing technique, long before it was in common use in TV studios. My makeup stayed pretty set for the whole day, but there was still a lot of preparation before the shows.

To get ready, we had a massive backstage dressing room where all our fixing up went on. There were rows of cosmetic tables with mirrors and portable wardrobes. It was controlled bedlam. Special hostesses were in charge of the dressing room, and they were quick to help anyone who lost a button or tore a hem or had a stuck zipper. The hairspray was so thick you could barely breathe.

There has been a lot written about the "tricks" contestants supposedly use to give themselves an edge: Vaseline on the teeth to widen the smile, glue spray on the butt to keep the swimsuit from riding up, Preparation H under the eyes to reduce swelling. I knew a little bit about some of the tricks, but as a pageant novice I hadn't really given any thought to actually trying them. I figured none of them would make me play the violin better or sound smarter in the interview, so I didn't do them. Later, when the reporter Penny Crone asked me which parts of me were real and which weren't, I have to say I was shocked. I'd been focusing on the substantive and *real* things I thought would actually help me win Miss America.

People always ask me if I made friends during the pageant or if it's a cutthroat competitive environment. Frankly, people have the idea that when women compete it's either a catfight or a lovefest. I would say neither is true. It was a *competition*. Think of any other competition. When you watch the Super Bowl, you aren't thinking, "I hope those guys love each other and become friends for life." Nor is there any mention of the male equivalent of catfighting. They're just competing. But when women are involved, the standard seems to be different.

As I saw it, if you really wanted to win Miss America, you might not be Miss Congeniality. (Only one Miss Congeniality, Vonda Kay Van Dyke, in 1965, ever won Miss America.) Not that you weren't a nice person. But you had to have a laser focus, and that could be construed as being aloof. I'm the most outgoing person you'll find, but in a competitive atmosphere, I don't get sidelined by distractions.

At the end of swimsuit and talent nights, all of the contestants gathered onstage and the highest scorer was announced. When my name was called as the winner of the talent competition on my preliminary night, I was deeply satisfied—aware that I was almost halfway there. I thought about how it was my talent that started me on this road, and I was exactly where I wanted to be.

By the day of the pageant I was exhausted and wound up as tight as a violin string. I had performed in front of large crowds for most of my life, and in my youth when I stepped onto a stage to give a violin performance I always felt confident and completely at ease. Now there were too many elements that were beyond my control. My talent win gave me confidence, but there were several other hurdles—assuming I made it into the top ten.

I saw my family at seven in the morning for the last time before being whisked away to the convention center where we were locked in all day. My mom met me in the lobby of the hotel. She hugged me and, holding my shoulders, looked me in the eye. "You can do this," she said. "You know how hard you worked for it."

Looking into my mom's eyes I had a flashback of all the times over the years when we'd been in similar situations together. I realized how much I relied on her for her unwavering support and love. I hugged her tight, tearing up with emotion. It would be a long day without her by my side, but having her there that early morning was just what I needed.

Then it was off to the convention center for a final day of grueling rehearsals. We worked on our production numbers all day, broke for a quick dinner, and then had hours to get ready. There was a lot of sitting around waiting, which wasn't so good for jangled nerves.

The 1989 Miss America pageant opened with Miss America 1988, Kaye Lani Rae Rafko, strolling across a college campus, young students walking in the background, welcoming viewers with an introduction about giving women opportunity. She was a wonderful exemplar for all of us, a registered nurse who was passionate about hospice care and dedicated to pursuing her career.

Then the announcer boomed the welcome to the Miss America pageant, "starring fifty-one talented and progressive women who've got success!" And we launched into our choreographed number.

After that, the top ten finalists were announced. When my name was called it was an enormous relief. I didn't have time then to think about the contestants who didn't make it, but later I reflected on what a blow it must have been for them. After months and even years of hard work, they were basically watching the pageant from backstage, with occasional appearances for production numbers. They had to keep those smiles pasted on their faces, even though they knew that for them the pageant was over. It was impressive to me how they kept their poise and spirit, even in defeat. A couple of years ago I was doing a live spot at the pageant with the women who had not made the top ten. I said into the camera that these women would go on to excel in many ways, and that one day one of them might even become president of the United States—to which Miss Nevada, standing nearby, called out, "Sign me up!" The number one question I get asked as a former Miss America is whether or not the pageant is still relevant today. And I say, "Of course," because the contestants are some of the smartest, talented, and most driven young women in America.

For me the highlight of the pageant was the talent competition—the one event where I felt completely confident, especially after winning the preliminary. I wore my elaborate (but inexpensive) green dress purchased so many months earlier in Canton, Ohio. Before I went onstage, I closed my eyes and said the Lord's Prayer, thinking of Grandma Hyllengren and feeling her presence strongly, as I always did at important times of my life. That moment of prayer and reflection put me in a state of peace. And once I was onstage, the pressure and nervousness faded away and I lost myself in the music.

I was playing a portion from *Zigeunerweisen* (*Gypsy Airs*) by Pablo de Sarasate. My parents and I had spent countless hours perfecting the exact cuts for the performance because the piece was eight minutes long and I only had three and a half minutes to perform. Our goal was to showcase the three parts that would most impress the judges and the audience. I opened with a flourish to pull the audience in, then transitioned to the slow, melodic—hopefully mesmerizing—part to show my passion and emotion. I finished with a fast, upbeat, difficult part. I wanted the audience with me, because judging is subjective, and it was important for the judges to experience the excitement of the audience.

I knew I had everyone spellbound during the middle, slow part of my performance, because you could hear a pin drop in the huge convention hall. My eyes burned with the start of tears, and they weren't tears of sadness. As an artist I often teared up while I was playing, because the music was so haunting and beautiful. It was all a way of pulling out the most amazing passion and sound to captivate my listeners. Finally, during the fast and furious part of the performance I could hear the audience start to clap again and almost say "Wow" with their voices. A smile now came over my face as I was nearing the end of what had gotten me started—my violin. I had done it. I had shown that a true violinist, trained classically, could come to the Miss America stage and wow the crowd. Thank you, God.

At the end of my performance, when I bowed deeply, I thought my hair accessory was falling off, so I grabbed it and yanked it off. Turned out it wasn't as loose as I thought it was, so I had to pull hard. I had a hairpiece on underneath, and I shuddered to think that I could have easily yanked off a hunk of hair along with the accessory as the finale to my performance. That would have made headlines!

I was nervous about the swimsuit competition, and I'm sure I wasn't the only one. It was the one event of the pageant that naturally inspired dread. Although I had practiced "the walk" many times, I couldn't get rid of the images of me stumbling on the stage, or the thought that close-ups of my butt would be seen on millions of TV screens. To make matters much worse, right before the swimsuit competition I got my period and had to rush around looking for a tampon. As I realized with horror that the string was dangling down, I grabbed a pair of scissors and cut it off. Moments later, I was walking onto the stage, trying to exude complete confidence in my rose-colored swimsuit.

Surprisingly, what turned out to be the most difficult moment was standing on the stage in my evening gown answering the question put to me by Gary Collins. He stood beside me and read from his card. "Miss Minnesota," he said, "there's much discussion of the influence of media in the political process. How do you feel about this issue?"

We had to stand really close to each other for the right camera angle, and I was short even in my high heels, so my eyes were level with Gary's teeth. I was transfixed by his big, gorgeous, *very* white teeth. I blanked for a second and I didn't really hear the question. I thought to myself, "I can't ask Gary to restate the question on live television in front of millions of people." So in a millisecond, with all those nervous thoughts in my head, I answered—and not very well. "I feel that being brought up with a moral background . . . and I was lucky enough to have a lot of values . . . that I would feel strong enough in my own decisions that the media would not disrupt any of my decisions in the political realm."

After my response I continued walking down the runway, look- ing for my parents in the audience, wanting to give them a thumbs- down. I thought I had blown the whole thing with my answer, but there wasn't time to wallow in my disappointment because imme- diately we were back onstage. I will say, though, that to this day I've never watched a video of myself giving that answer.

The longest twelve minutes of my life were spent on live national television, in front of an audience of millions, wearing a blue sequined gown, convinced that I had just lost the Miss America pageant.

It was the end of the night, the moment of truth. The ten of us were lined up on the stage, holding hands, waiting for the panel of celebrity judges seated in an orchestra pit below us to hand Gary their verdict. Suddenly it became clear that something was very wrong. From my perspective on the stage I watched what the audi- ence and viewers at home couldn't see—the judges were scrambling around frantically. They were in a panic, flipping through a pro-gram book that listed all the contestants, six on each spread.

Gary Collins walked over to the edge of the stage, thinking they would hand him the results. "May I have the decision, please," he said. There was a furious consultation and he reeled back. "You have a *what*?" he cried. "A *tie*? Can you believe this?"

Shock rocked the hall, and we stood in the spotlight, not know-ing what would happen. I looked down at the judges and saw them flip to the spread with my picture. I knew exactly where my picture was on the page, and I could see it even from way up on the stage. Someone pointed to my picture in the book. And then the crushing blow. They all shook their heads, *no*. I sucked in a breath and fought to keep my smile in place. My eyes searched the audience for my mother; she would let me know that everything was okay. But I couldn't find her. So I began to think about what I would do to be a graceful loser—how I could breathe meaning into a year of the most incredible effort I had ever made. All my hard work—the dieting, the brutal exercise regimen, the humiliating swimsuit fit-tings, the endless mock interviews, the violin practice—had come down to this. In that moment, I was convinced that I was doing the thing I hated most in the world. I was losing.

When Gary announced that there was a tie, we naturally as-sumed that it was between the winner and the first runner-up. It turns out the tie was between the third and fourth runner-up. But those twelve minutes were a lifetime. And I spent most of them thinking I was toast.

To make matters worse, Gary was desperately trying to fill the time. We were on live TV and we couldn't just stand there. So he started asking us more questions. He asked me what I would have done differently—which I thought was the kind of question you ask people who lose. I cringed and said that I would have answered my question better. I thought I'd blown it with my answer, and I was dying inside.

I knew one thing. I had no choice about whether I was picked, but I did have a choice about how I reacted. I decided I was going to accept loss with a positive attitude—not be devastated by it as I had been when I'd lost Miss T.E.E.N. I told myself it had taken a lot of guts to get up there, no matter what the outcome. As those moments passed, I was having the biggest learning experience of my life. I realized that after all my incredibly hard work, I had still won no matter what happened.

The minutes ticked by. Gary and his cohost wife, Mary Ann Mobley, were getting increasingly desperate for things to say as the judges reballoted. It was excruciating. We were like statues on the stage, frozen in place, clutching hands. Smiling on the outside, wilting on the inside.

Finally, at long last, the judges were ready. Gary read the results: Fourth runner-up, Miss Alabama. Third runner-up, Miss California. Second runner-up, Miss Oklahoma.

There were seven of us remaining, and only two of the seven would be picked. So near and yet so far.

And then he called my name and, a beat later, Maya Walker, Miss Colorado. The final two.

As I was walking to the center of the stage I saw Kaye Lani standing in the corner. Our eyes met, and she gave me the tiniest nod. I didn't think she knew anything (and that turned out to be the case), but I took the nod as an encouragement—her way of saying it was going to be okay.

To the side I was aware of a flurry of white—my hometown fans waving their white hankies. The idea of the hankies came from the Minnesota Twins, who had won the World Series in 1987. The team had Homer Hankies that the fans would wave, so we produced some for the pageant, and my family and friends from Minnesota waved them wildly every time my name was called.

Maya and I hugged each other, and she cried emotionally, "Oh, Gretchen!" The only thing I could think of to say was, "I can't believe they picked the two shortest ones." We were both stunned.

Gary played it out. "Now there are two—just two," he announced solemnly. "I mentioned earlier tonight ninety thousand are involved in the pageant, and it's come down to two. One of you is going to receive a $17,000 scholarship. You will also be Miss America's standby. First runner-up is still pretty sensational." He paused. "But now one of you is going to have her life changed dramatically, forever, from this moment on it will never be the same."

Another pause. Then, "The first runner-up . . . is Maya Walker. Miss America is Gretchen Carlson!"

I burst into tears and mouthed "thank you" to the judges.

People always ask me what I felt at the moment I became Miss America. I wish I could say. It was all a blur of emotion. Later I heard criticism because I crossed my arms and it was interpreted as "hugging myself"—as if I was full of myself. Really. Truth is, the sense of relief was so intense—almost impossible to describe. But that was just the beginning of how my every little move would be analyzed to death.

Before I could even catch my breath, someone put a rose-covered stick in my hands, which I later learned was a scepter. Shows you what a novice I was. Kaye Lani was there behind me pinning the crown on my head. By the way, that crown doesn't go on so easily, and there's no guarantee that it will stay on. In 1970, when Phyllis George won, her crown fell off her head right on the stage, rhinestones splattering all over the place. She walked down the runway holding it in her hand! After that they wisely sewed in elastic pieces in the shape of a T so that the crown could easily be bobby-pinned into place. However, when I won Miss Minnesota they used duct tape. When the outgoing Miss Minnesota went to put the crown on my head she accidentally stuck it too far down on my forehead instead of on the top of my head. I couldn't help giggling coming down the runway and imagining what it looked like.

I started walking down the runway, waving and crying, and the Miss America theme song was playing. I felt my mascara running in rivers down my cheeks. (Waterproof mascara, anyone?) Halfway down, I spotted BeBe Shopp, the first Miss America from Minnesota, 1948, now in her sixties, running alongside the runway, cheering. It was incredibly emotional seeing her. I grinned and gave her a thumbs-up. (The other Miss America from Minnesota, Dorothy Benham, 1977, would have been there, but she was giving birth to her daughter that night in a Connecticut hospital.)

It was all lovely and romantic, but behind the scenes there were other considerations. For one thing there was a Disney World commercial to shoot. The "I'm Going to Disney World" spot was an advertising campaign that first aired after the 1987 Super Bowl. New York Giants quarterback Phil Simms was shown stopping in the middle of the celebration to answer an announcer's question, "Where are you going now that you've won the Super Bowl?" His response: "I'm going to Disney World!" They made a deal to do the commercial at Miss America, and we were all coached in advance.

Of course I forgot as I was coming back up the runway, and they were yelling at me, "Gretchen Carlson, you've just become Miss America, where are you going now?" Finally I realized I was supposed to say, "I'm going to Disney World!" It was the last time the commercial was ever aired at the Miss America pageant, although it's still used in football and baseball, and Nancy Kerrigan did the spot with her Olympic silver medal for ice skating in 1994.

When I finally got backstage, two nice ladies took charge of me and led me to a chair. When I sat down, the first thing they asked was if I wanted smelling salts. I thought that was so quaint. I had heard of people getting smelling salts when they fainted. Wow! I didn't feel like I was going to faint—at least not yet. I casually said I would pass on the kind offer.

Meanwhile, they were fluttering around me, fixing my eye makeup, because my next stop was the press room.

They took me down, and what seemed like a hundred photographers mobbed me, yelling, "Miss America, here, here, over here!" I was in a fog, and I had no idea who they were talking to until I realized, "Oh, yeah, that's me. Miss America is *me!*" Then I went on to a room full of reporters. I stepped up to the podium, and they barraged me with questions. No surprise, I didn't have prepared remarks. I babbled thanks to everyone, and fortunately it didn't last too long. I was completely beside myself by that point.

Finally, my family crowded into the room. Dad was crying, of course, and Mom was beaming. She hugged me. "I knew you would do it!" she cried, and she really meant it. She *had* known all along. Kurt and Molly were at the pageant, but I couldn't see them yet. I later learned that they were in the bathroom crying their eyes out. My grandfather was there with his second wife, smiling proudly and calling out, "Sparkles!" Kris came up and threw her arms around me. We were both sobbing. It was a very emotional moment.

Afterward, with the clock ticking toward 1:00 a.m., I was swept away through the back kitchen of the casino, still wearing my gown and crown and clutching my scepter. They brought me to a reception of all the contestants and their families, where I spoke briefly before getting into a limo to ride back to my hotel. I was staying at Resorts International, which was owned by Merv Griffin. Merv, who was excited that I was staying at his hotel, acted quickly, along with his companion Eva Gabor, to set up a pizza party for me and my family in the presidential suite, and they joined us there. Behind the scenes, all of my things had been moved from my regular room, and I'd be sleeping in that lavish suite for my first night as Miss America. Not that I got much sleep.

By the time everyone left, it was 3:00 a.m., and I was dead tired but running on adrenaline. I looked at myself in the mirror and said, "Oh my gosh. You did it." I thought back to the previous morning when I'd been a nervous wreck, and now it was all over, and I felt indescribably thrilled. But I was also thinking, somewhat petrified, "Now what?" I'd been so focused on getting there that I hadn't given any thought to what the year was actually going to be. It stretched ahead like a great, terrifying, exhilarating adventure.

CHAPTER 5

American Womanhood 101

What is the first thing Miss America does when she wakes up the morning after the pageant? Jumps in the Atlantic Ocean! I'm not kidding.

I'd heard about this tradition and seen the pictures in newspapers of previous Miss Americas jumping in the waves, but I hadn't really thought about it. Now I had to do my first big photo shoot and it was only 7:30 in the morning. I put on shorts and a top and went out to the boardwalk where a gang of photographers was waiting for me. It was a chilly September morning, and I shivered.

I immediately felt insecure. The photographers were gruff, ordering me to leap in the waves, which might have been a fine idea for a tall, long-legged person, but I was having a hard time lifting my short legs above the water. The photographers were not amused.

They wanted the cheesecake shot, and they became frustrated with my graceless efforts. "Hey," they yelled, "you gotta jump higher! Higher! No, no, higher!" I thought of Kaye Lani, my five-foot-ten predecessor, and was sure she'd done a beautiful job of jumping in the waves. I had a big smile pasted on my face, but inside I was thinking, "Seven hours as Miss America, and already I'm blowing it."

They wanted a shot of me on the beach doing some kind of victory leap. I jumped a couple of times, and one photographer called out, "Can't you do better than that?" I took a deep breath and thought, "Here goes!" and I jumped as high as I could with my legs folded behind me like a cheerleader. The newspaper caption called it "a joyous leap." Phew! I did it. I'll tell you a secret: To this day, in spite of having done hundreds of photo shoots in my life, for Miss America and in television, it still doesn't come naturally to me. I always feel awkward posing for the camera. I would have made a terrible model!

I was relieved when it was finally over. I quickly dressed in a pink St. John knit dress I'd borrowed from my mom and went to meet the press. This was my first big interview, and I hadn't been coached. I was just being myself. I told them I was an overachiever. I told them I didn't carry any good-luck charms to the pageant and my win wasn't luck but hard work. I told them about my brothers calling me Blimpo and the Hindenburg when I was a kid. It was all fodder for the headlines. When they asked me what kind of Miss America I'd make, I laughed and replied, "A short one." I learned quickly that every single word out of my mouth would be pored over for meaning, and the most unflattering depictions would make it into the headlines—"New Miss America Confesses She Was a Teen Blimpo." They loved that one!

I didn't even stop for breakfast, and I should have been entitled to a big spread after nine months of dieting. But I didn't eat much at all my first week as Miss America. The schedule was too packed. The first time I remember actually gorging on food was a night in New Hampshire alone in my hotel room a week later when I ate an entire box of gingersnap cookies.

After my press conference, I said goodbye to my family, which was a wrenching experience. I was already insecure about my ocean frolic and was overwhelmed with the feeling that I didn't know what I was doing. I was now losing my rock and foundation, knowing I wouldn't see them until my "homecoming" in Anoka in a month. It was a tearful parting. I then got into a limo and headed to New York for an intensive week of media appearances. There was a lot going on, including choosing a wardrobe for the year. People are always curious about where I got my clothes for my time as Miss America. Thankfully, I didn't have to come up with them on my own. The pageant had an arrangement with the Crafted with Pride in U.S.A. Council, an organization that supported clothing made in the United States, to supply my wardrobe. They brought racks of clothing to my hotel, and an assistant was there to help me pick out outfits. Immediately there was a problem because I was petite. The clothing had been selected before the pageant, with the assumption that Miss America would be taller, so a lot of the items didn't fit right. Every petite woman in America knows what I'm talking about! Later, they sent some boxes of petite clothes, and that was great.

The pageant also sent in a couple of women who gave me advice about how to write speeches and develop talking points. They coached me about doing interviews. That would turn out to be absolutely crucial training, because now I was in the public eye.

My first night in New York, bleary-eyed, I met Leonard Horn and Kaye Lani for a late dinner. I was very conscious that I had to get up at the crack of dawn to appear on *Today* for an interview by Deborah Norville. It was going to be another short night.

Early in the morning, the renowned hairdresser Vincent arrived to do my hair and makeup. Vincent was so famous that he was known by his first name alone, and he served as a consultant to the Miss America pageant. When he was young he'd styled hair for the likes of Audrey Hepburn, Grace Kelly, and Judy Garland. He'd even been called on to style Jackie Kennedy's hair. He was also Diane Sawyer's longtime hairdresser and still is. Vincent was amazing—and he made me look totally different than I looked when I won. Using his Velcro roller technique, he smoothed my hair out in a simple flattering bob that was sleek and sophisticated, and much more natural than my hairstyle at the pageant. Not so much hairspray and teasing. I loved the look. I was now more like the girl next door than a glamorous queen.

I've already recounted my torturous first press conference in the Big Apple, with the reporter Penny Crone trying to trip me up, followed by an uncomfortable interview with Jack Cafferty where he tried hard to attribute my win to "luck." These press encounters tested my mettle, but I was pleased to see that the verdict in the wider media was that I'd handled the rudeness gracefully. I have to say that in general, reporters across America treated me pretty well. Usually they were interested in hearing what I had to say and knowing about my journey. Looking back at the headlines from that year, the majority of them stressed my credentials, my violin performances, and the fact that we were in a new era, where Miss America was judged for who she was, not what she looked like.

I had a big personality as a baby.
| *David Bank Studios, MN*

Living in the Halloween capital of the world and being a ham, I dressed as a pumpkin one year.

My parents were a stunning couple. The car was pretty cool too!

Four generations of women: Grandma Berenice Hyllengren, Kris, mom, me, and my maternal great grandmother Nora Newstrom (Gramsie).

I had a special connection with my grandfather, who called me "Sparkles."

I loved my softball team, the Lincoln Logs. Mom was the coach, and I played second base.

Playing a violin solo with the Minnesota Orchestra was a thrilling event for a thirteen-year-old. Once I started to play, I didn't feel nervous, only euphoric.

Mary West and Ken Davenport gave me the gift of the violin.

After full days of work at Aspen, Hope Easton and I played for tourists at night and made a little money.

I wore my prom dress and won Miss T.E.E.N. Minnesota. Later, I was first runner-up at the nationals.

The violin was my secret weapon in winning Miss America.

The moments after being crowned Miss America were a blur. Here I am beginning the famous walk. | *Courtesy of the Miss America Organization*

Eva Gabor, a judge at the pageant, told me I could have been her daughter. She took me shopping on Rodeo Drive in her fancy car.

As Miss America I was privileged to meet President Reagan at the White House. | *The White House*

My precious children, Kaia
and Christian. Kaia was
delighted to be a big sister.

My wedding day, October 4,
1997, was perfect in every
way. | *Joan Buccina, Buccina Studios*

My last public violin performance
at a Texas Rangers game while
working at KXAS in Dallas.
That's Casey in the background.
| *Texas Rangers Baseball Club*

I had a front-row seat for Fox at the royal wedding, when Kate Middleton made her entrance.

A first for cable news. I went on air without makeup to present a positive role model for young girls.

My parents continue to attend the Miss America pageant with me every year. I love being on the Miss America Organization board and sharing this experience with them.

Fox & Friends, my home for seven years, in the middle between Steve Doocy and Brian Kilmeade.
| *Courtesy of Fox News Channel*

On the set of my show, *The Real Story with Gretchen Carlson*.

Support for the troops is an important issue for me.

| Courtesy of Fox News Channel

Dogsledding in Alaska: a memorable experience, definitely outside our family's comfort zone, but worth it!

Those headlines didn't always filter down to the public perception, but it was a step in the right direction.

One of the first big decisions was whether I'd go on Johnny Carson or David Letterman. You couldn't do both. Leonard Horn was pushing for Carson, because, as the story went, Letterman hadn't been so nice to previous Miss Americas. I also favored Carson because he allowed people to perform, and I wanted to play my violin on *The Tonight Show*.

But Letterman was really working for it. Every night he put a stool in the middle of the stage and placed a violin on it. He'd tell the audience, "She's coming, folks. She'll be here. Don't worry. I'm going to get Miss America."

The pageant finally relented and agreed to do Letterman. In spite of the violin on the chair, Letterman didn't have musical performances on his show, so I was disappointed I wouldn't be displaying my talent. I was on the same night as Julia Child, who was dozing in the green room when I arrived. She went on after me for a cooking demonstration with Dave. The idea was to make hamburgers, but when the cooking element didn't work, she quickly changed it to steak tartare. It was a very funny segment.

When I walked out on the stage the first thing I said was, "Where's the violin?" Letterman said he thought I was bringing my own, which was back at the hotel. He wasn't serious about me playing. It was a talk show and we talked. He revealed that he had a sister named Gretchen. At one point he asked me, "When you're on the road, if a guy comes up to you and asks, 'Would you like to have dinner?' could you go out to dinner with him?"

"I don't think so," I said. "But I don't really know, actually. It hasn't happened yet."

"I'm sure it's going to happen a lot," he said, grinning wickedly. Then, "Would you like to have dinner?" That got a huge laugh.

Frankly, I kept waiting for him to be mean or sarcastic, but he couldn't have been nicer. I was surprised that I felt so comfortable schmoozing with Dave.

At first I liked my label as "the smart Miss America," but I soon realized that it meant being tested at every turn. Within a week, I had my biggest test ever. I was in Denver when Gary Collins and Mary Ann Mobley invited me to appear with them on a live TV show to promote a new type of satellite device called "Miss America." The broadcast would be beamed to a convention of five thousand engineers and executives in Washington, D.C.

What I didn't know was that we were filming a segment of the show *Super Bloopers and Practical Jokes*, hosted by Ed McMahon and Dick Clark. I was the unwitting foil.

It was in my nature to be prepared, so before the event while they were doing my makeup, I kept asking questions about the device and how it worked. No one had any answers. In fact, everyone acted nervous when I asked questions. I think they were worried that I had somehow found out that I was being set up. But that was not the case.

Gary, Mary Ann, and I took the stage next to the odd-looking contraption. Everything was fine. But shortly before we were scheduled to start broadcasting, Gary was called offstage to answer a phone call. Then Mary Ann left to fix her broken microphone. As I was waiting for them to get back, the segment director suddenly told me that the broadcast was starting early. "Just ad-lib for a couple of minutes until Gary gets back," he said. Sure, I could do that. I gave a nice little speech about being Miss America and how pleased I was to be there introducing this new machine.

Still no Gary.

"Talk about the system," the director whispered.

"I don't know anything about the system," I whispered back. But I kept ad-libbing, trying to describe the machine in front of me.

"Gary will be coming," he promised. "Here, we have cue cards."

Well, that was a relief, but the guy was holding the cue cards upside down. I read them anyway, and I must say I did a flawless job—and then he dropped them, scattering them all over the floor. I didn't miss a beat, just kept reading off the floor. I thought I must have looked incredibly stupid and nervous. It was absolute torture. So many thoughts were racing through my head. Here I was, barely Miss America, and now they were probably going to fire me. I was supposed to be the smart Miss America! What a laugh. I felt my heart pounding in my chest as I realized that all of my hard work to become Miss America was literally on the line. I felt such anxiety and desperation.

Finally, after this had gone on for an excruciating length of time, Gary and Mary Ann appeared on the stage. They told me to press a button on the machine, and Ed McMahon's voice boomed out, "Gretchen, you're on *Super Bloopers and Practical Jokes*."

I collapsed laughing, but I was kind of sobbing too. I cried, "I want my mommy!"

I didn't like being tricked that way. What I didn't realize at first was that my unflappable performance was actually a selling point, showing I wouldn't melt under pressure. After the show aired six months later, I received calls from two different TV agents asking if I'd ever thought about doing television. They said, "If you can do that, you're a natural." Later I included the *Bloopers* tape on my professional reel when I was looking for jobs in television, and ironically, it became a point in my favor.

Right after the *Bloopers* show, I was on the road in Atlanta to attend a dinner for one of the sponsors. There were two thousand people in the hall. I sat at the head table and we ate dinner, and it was delightful. Then, right before dessert was served, a guy came up behind me and whispered, "I just want to give you a five-minute warning for your keynote."

I turned around. "Excuse me?"

"Your keynote," he repeated.

"Oh, yes," I mumbled. Nobody had told me I'd be giving a keynote address. "How long would you like me to speak?"

"Thirty-five or forty minutes." In other words, a *lifetime.*

I grabbed a cocktail napkin and excused myself from the table and went into the bathroom. I had five minutes to write down a bulleted list, and I tried to remember the talking points my coaches had given me.

I gave the speech, and to this day I can't remember what I talked about, but they applauded enthusiastically, so I guess I did okay. It was a great lesson. From that moment on I didn't go anywhere without having at least three speeches ready. But it also gave me confidence. That and the *Bloopers* experience showed me I could perform under duress, and that was a quality I needed, because every day of being Miss America presented another unexpected challenge. I was called upon to deal with the public in ways that most twenty-two-year-olds would never face. I had performed my whole life, so I could do it, but now, I thought, I was developing as a person. I felt much older than my age. I'd been in many scary and tough situations before—violin competitions, being on my own in Aspen—and I'd learned how to dig deep to find a sense of confidence. I found comfort in something that was said to me the day after I won: "You weren't necessarily the most polished person on the stage, but you were the most refreshing." I took that to heart.

I have to admit I suffered a tremendous amount of self-doubt that year. Yes, I knew I was smart and talented, but the little voice never went away: How was I stacking up against other Miss Americas? I'm not talking about looks—sure, I was short and I couldn't change that. The truth is, Miss America is an icon, but each of us is unique, and people don't always appreciate that. They see the icon, and they fill it with unrealistic expectations. In the years since being Miss America, I've learned from other winners that those feelings of self-doubt and inadequacy weren't exclusive to me. It's a big role to fill.

When you're crowned Miss America, you immediately go up on a pedestal. Young girls look at you and think you've achieved everything you ever dreamed of—that it's the pinnacle of your life and not just the beginning. They think you're unapproachable and far above what they could ever hope for. That's not what I wanted young girls to see when they looked at me.

I was trying to be real, to be myself, to show my flaws, which is why I talked about being overweight as a child. I wanted young women and girls to look at me and think, "If she could do it, I can too." That's the essence of being a role model. I believe that every child is born with a gift, and it just needs to be cultivated from the inside out. Later, when I had a daughter, I didn't even tell her I'd been Miss America. Kaia found out from someone else when she was eight. I was conscious of not wanting her to feel that she had to live up to something so big before she'd had a chance to build her own sense of self. I realized from experience that self-esteem is hard won and easily shaken by the realities of the world around you. The fact that I could still feel insecure as Miss America was proof of that.

I was also dealing with an unfamiliar level of fame. Our culture loves celebrity, and we give it liberally to people, whether they're worthy or not. The biggest shock is when it lands on you overnight. One day no one knows your name. The next day, everyone does. I was grateful that my upbringing gave me such a solid grounding and an understanding of what matters and what doesn't. The fame never went to my head. Even so, the enormous notoriety of being Miss America was quite an adjustment. People came out of the woodwork, claiming they had dated me or were related to me. I discovered many cousins, seven times removed! My family was also under siege. In the early weeks my parents' phone in Anoka was ringing off the hook, and they were completely inexperienced in handling the press. They trusted everyone. Big mistake. One day a reporter and a cameraman appeared on their doorstep claiming to be from the London *Times*. My parents invited them in, gave them a tour of the house, and let them take pictures. The next day the pictures were splashed across the front page of the *National Enquirer,* not the London *Times*. They included some very personal and private photographs of our family and our bedrooms. My parents had been hoodwinked. They had expected a certain level of respect that the paparazzi did not recognize. The stress of sudden fame included the realization that there were eyes and ears everywhere, and they weren't necessarily trustworthy. The experience made me a little bit jaded, a little more cautious than I'd been before, and that distrust has always stayed with me. Even a public person has a right to personal space, and I protect mine.

Fortunately, a month into being Miss America, I had an emotional and spiritual reprieve—my official "homecoming" trip to Anoka. It didn't come a moment too soon. Until I saw my family, I was beginning to wilt under the tremendous pressure. To win, I had visualized becoming Miss America, but my visualization ended at the runway. Being thrown into the status of a celebrity, literally overnight, with no preparation about how to *be* Miss America, is tough. Home with my family I could relax for the first time—even if it was only for a day. I cherished the reminder of my small-town values and the upbringing that had nurtured me.

Anoka had declared a Gretchen Carlson Day, which included a parade down Main Street and a balloon launch at Lincoln Elementary School, followed by a violin performance at the high school and a reception at Zion Lutheran Church. Ten thousand people came out to the parade, cramming the streets and reaching out to shake my hand as the car slowly edged forward. I saw "We love you, Gretchen" written in chalk along the parade route. At the elementary school, the kids had been there since early morning preparing for the balloon launch. An additional five thousand people crowded into the Anoka High School field house where I gave my violin performance.

The reception at Zion was a five-dollar-a-head benefit to establish a scholarship for an Anoka High School student who excelled academically and in the arts. The food was great. It turned out that earlier someone had asked me what my idea of paradise was, and I'd answered, "An endless buffet of Leeann Chin's foods," referring to the famous restaurant chain in Minneapolis whose buffets I loved. When Leeann Chin heard what I said, she offered to supply a selection of appetizers for the reception, including all of my favorites. So I got my wish.

I also autographed pictures at Main Motors and enjoyed chatting with all my neighbors and friends. America is a big country, and people who didn't know me were forming instant impressions. But here I was *known*. It was just the kind of day I needed to restore my spirits, to remind me where I came from and how much the love and values of my hometown meant to me.

Being Miss America was the *fullest* full-time job I've ever had. I was on the road every single day of the year, except for six days off at Christmas and four at Easter. Many people think being Miss America is glamorous, but glamour is probably the last word I'd use to describe my nonstop schedule. I traveled about twenty-five thousand miles a month, landing in about five different cities every week. By year's end I had visited 240 cities. After I won, Kaye Lani joked to me, "Gretchen, the minute you feel this starts to be a burden to you, the minute you want to quit, don't worry, because if they can't find someone else, I'll take over the spot and go another year." She was trying to say that although it was arduous, she had loved it and was even sad to see it end. I thought about her words often, because it was true that I was constantly moved by the amazing reception I received across the country and grateful for the opportunity to meet so many incredible people. It more than made up for the strenuous schedule. Still, I think most Miss Americas are ready to pass along the crown at the end of the year.

One of the biggest surprises for me—and the real beauty of it—was discovering that the Miss America Organization was a homespun, grassroots organization. My appearances were booked through the office in Atlantic City, where one lone guy, Bob Bryan, the business manager, handled all the details. Before I was even chosen, Bob had booked appearances for three months solid, with the remaining months filling up by the day. I was scheduled for charity and civic events, fund-raisers, autograph sessions, conventions, club luncheons, parades, visits to children's and veterans' hospitals, and speeches to student groups. I also did commercial and sponsor appearances, for which I was paid a fee.

For example, Gillette was a pageant sponsor, so I toured their facilities in Boston for two days and met all the people on the factory lines. I also went to drugstores all over America and signed autographs on behalf of Gillette for several hours each stop. Afterward I often had dinner with the executives from those stores. In between I did local TV and radio interviews. Then I was on a plane the next morning. My schedule was packed, but the perks were amazing. I was driven everywhere in stretch limousines, and there were always flowers—huge bouquets of flowers. The roses I got that year could have filled a florist's warehouse.

I also got to rub shoulders with some pretty famous people. I soon learned that everyone wanted to meet Miss America, including people I had once only admired from afar. It was a thrill to go to the White House to meet President Reagan. He was absolutely charming, and, noting that I was a student at Stanford, he remarked, "Stanford is getting too liberal." He loved California, though. It was his home, and I think because I went to school there he considered me a little bit Californian. I hobnobbed with the iconic golfer Arnold Palmer (my dad's hero), hockey phenom Wayne Gretzky, and country music legend Glen Campbell. I was especially touched to receive a gift from Louise Mandrell—a violin-shaped case with a bottle of champagne. I still have that case.

I always traveled with a companion, an older woman hired by

the pageant. There were two of them, alternating every other month. My first was Ellie Ross, who was a seasoned veteran in her early sixties, an old pro. She'd grown up in Atlantic City and lived nearby her whole life. She was a huge pageant enthusiast and a volunteer for many years. Most people don't realize that the Miss America system is built on volunteers, but it's a remarkable fact. There are few paid people in the system. In 1977 someone asked Ellie if she'd like a job as a traveling companion. Her daughter was grown and her marriage was ending so she said yes, and she'd been traveling with Miss America ever since. By the time she got to me she'd seen it all. She used to talk about the prayer she said every year at the Miss America pageant: "Dear Lord, I don't care what state she represents. It doesn't matter what her talent is or if she's blonde or brunette. Just let her be easy to live with."

I quickly realized that I couldn't have managed without Ellie. She was more than a chaperone. She was a coordinator who took care of all the details—and there were many, many details. More important, she was an enforcer, who got me in and out of appearances without ruffling feathers. When it was time to go, she'd announce it, and there was no arguing. I was grateful that I didn't have to be the one to call the autograph sessions to a close. I probably would have ended up staying long into the night. Being Miss America's traveling companion was a very challenging role, but as Ellie once quipped, "We haven't lost one yet."

We had adjoining rooms in hotels, and Ellie was supposed to help me get dressed, but I sometimes ended up helping her get dressed, because she often couldn't reach her zipper. We were quite a pair. I was helping her and she was helping me. She had amazing stories of her adventures. She actually tried to write a book, which she planned to call *Queen Mother,* but she said no publisher would buy it because "it didn't have any sex in it."

When we registered at hotels, both rooms were in Ellie's name to protect my identity. You can imagine the kinds of pranks people might play if they knew Miss America was staying at a hotel. My successor, Debbye Turner, tells the story of how some guy got up on her floor and knocked on her door, and she looked out of the peephole and he was totally nude.

On long nights alone, too tired to do anything else, Ellie and I sat in the hotel talking and playing gin rummy, although most of the time I played solitaire, which sometimes was a pretty good analogy for my life growing up and sometimes even as Miss America.

When we flew—always first class—Ellie made sure to collect a few miniature scotch bottles, and when we got to the hotel she'd mix herself a scotch with ice, avoiding the expense of hotel liquor.

Ellie hated that I traveled with my violin—well, not really, but it was kind of a pain. I also had four large pieces of luggage, but they were all checked, except the violin, which we had to cart through security. Ellie would grumble, "Why couldn't you play the piano?"

"Well, actually I do," I said.

"Oh, shut up," she said, rolling her eyes.

This was in the days before security was so strict, but every single time, I'd get pulled over and asked, "What's this?" Believe it or not, the most common joke among security guards was to ask, "You don't have a rifle in there, do you?" Goes to show how times have changed!

Ellie carried the crown, and it had to go through security too. Everyone wanted to look at the crown. In earlier years it had been placed in a cookie tin, but the rhinestones kept falling off, so now it was encased in a velvet-lined wooden box. We'd open the box and the other passengers in line would crane their heads to catch a glimpse of the famous crown.

My second companion, Anita Puhala, had only been on the job for a year. About halfway through my year she got sick, and I suggested that my mom could fill in as my companion for the month of May. The pageant was skeptical. They preferred having an impartial companion, fearing there would be fights if family members were involved. I just laughed. "Who better to fight with than my mother?" I said.

I was grateful that my mom was willing to step in. I didn't realize it at the time, but she later told me it was quite boring for her—sitting hour after hour while I signed autographs, gave speeches, shook hands. We both appreciated that people like Ellie were pros who deserved a lot of admiration. They loved the work. For them it wasn't an ordeal.

I called Bob Bryan frequently, cajoling him. "Bob, if there's a chance that on any of these appearances I can play my violin, that's what I want to do." He'd usually try to make it happen, and I was happy to have many opportunities to play. I played during the intermission at the Ice Capades. I played the national anthem for a Twins game in the Minneapolis Metrodome (which was demolished in 2014). I played at the Grady Gammage Memorial Auditorium in Tempe with the Phoenix Symphony. I played at the Ordway, the new auditorium in Saint Paul, as a soloist with my former Greater Twin Cities Youth Symphonies. I played at the Epcot Center at Disney World with a national youth orchestra. I played at schools. I played at VA hospitals. I played at big corporate events.

It was the highlight of my term and very important to me. I figured that if people doubted what the program was about, maybe I had a chance to change their minds with my music. And that actually happened.

I also gave more speeches than I can count, mostly motivational speeches to companies and at corporate events, where I talked about success and failure.

A big lesson of being Miss America was that I could never wake up on the wrong side of the bed. Every day people were meeting me for the first and probably only time, and that first impression would stick. Trust me, there were a lot of days I woke up exhausted and not feeling sociable, but I pulled myself together to go out and meet the public, because, after all, being Miss America was a once-in-a-lifetime, amazing opportunity.

I was humble about being Miss America, and it wasn't in my nature to seek out recognition. Once on a plane, I had my nose in a book when the man sitting next to me suddenly said, "You're Miss America, aren't you?" I whispered, "Yes, but please don't tell anyone." He snickered and looked at me unpleasantly. "I thought Miss America was supposed to be *nice.*"

I had to tread carefully because people had incredible expectations of who they thought Miss America should be. I remember one incident at a sponsor dinner when I had a couple of glasses of wine, and someone called the Miss America office and complained about me drinking. On another occasion I was wearing a pretty green dress and it was a bit low cut, and the guy in charge of the event called the pageant and complained about my "décolletage" being too exposed. I didn't even know what a décolletage was! I got a good laugh out of that. I realized that I was never going to please everybody, but it was still a surprise when people had negative impressions of me without even knowing who I was.

My dad's advice from my early life resonated with me. He said, "Gretchen, no matter how hard you try you're just never going to get everyone to like you; you're just not." It's good advice, and I often pass it on to young people when I give speeches today. It sounds simple, but you have to work on having that mind-set. If you're always focused on having everyone like you, it destroys your spontaneity and sense of self. So as Miss America I had to get a handle on that pretty quickly, because there were also plenty of people who just didn't like me because of my title. Some critics were quite open about saying I was part of a system that exploited women.

They made assumptions about me being a bimbo or a "beauty queen," totally ignoring who I actually was. It hurt, but I kept thinking I could change a few minds once people saw me, heard me play, and listened to me speak. That was my goal.

Some of the fans who came out to see me were disappointed for other reasons. They didn't think I looked like Miss America was supposed to look. People think you should appear just as if you walked off the runway that moment. Many times I'd be sitting at a table signing autographs, and I'd hear the conversation down the line. "Can you believe it? *That's* Miss America?" They must have thought I didn't have ears to hear them. Then they'd come up to the table and I'd give them my best smile: "Oh, hi, Sylvia. It's so great to see you. Sure I'll take a picture with you—here we go . . . cheese!" I got used to the comments and the harsh evaluations. It seemed that everyone's sister and girlfriend was better-looking than Miss America!

One thing I heard a lot was, "Where's your crown?" I didn't always wear it, especially if I was going to play my violin. I was worried that my spirited playing would knock the crown right off my head. I loved wearing the crown when I was signing autographs or visiting schools and hospitals, but I didn't like to wear it when I spoke at business events because I wanted people to focus on my words and not be distracted. I got some flak for that. In later years, the pageant guidelines would state that Miss America didn't need to wear the crown unless it was specifically stipulated. In fact, many of the official photographs of Miss America since my time have showed her holding the crown, not wearing it. I've always said that the Miss America pageant emulates where women are in society and has evolved with them. It's a work in progress, not just a historical artifact.

Many years later, I was doing a Mother's Day presentation for young women and mothers at a church in Texas, and the coordinator said, "Of course you'll bring your crown, right?"

I said, "Yeah, if I can find it."

She was shocked. "If you can *find* it? You don't know where your Miss America crown is?"

I had to confess that I wasn't sure. "Maybe in my mom's basement."

I looked at her face and realized that I was giving her great pain, so I quickly said, "Don't worry, I'll bring it."

Then I called my mom, a little bit panicked. "I've moved around so much, Mom, please tell me you have the crown!" She found it and saved the day.

Often at corporate events I was introduced with my vital statistics—even though I was about to give a serious speech about professional success. On one occasion, the man who spoke before me was a very accomplished executive, and his introduction was a tribute to his incredible credentials. When they got to me, the male emcee said, "And now we're honored to hear from this year's Miss America. She's a five-foot-three, 108-pound gal with green eyes hailing from the state of Minnesota." No mention of my name, no mention of my background, no mention of anything pertinent except my vitals.

When I got up, I said, "As you can see, there are unfortunately those who do not yet understand that being Miss America embodies more than just vital statistics." I so wished he'd introduced me as a classical violinist. I so wished he'd said I was an honor student at Stanford. I so wished he'd said Miss America was the largest scholarship pageant for women in the world. I was trying to stand up for myself, Miss America, and all women, but sometimes my words sounded more frustrated than eloquent. At the end of my year, I proposed adding GPA to the scoring in some small way because so many of the contestants excelled academically. In my mind it could be a way to stop the critics' constant analysis that Miss America was only a beauty pageant while drawing more attention to the scholarship aspect of the program. I figured we should celebrate the brains behind the beauty.

Whenever I could I challenged the stereotype, but it was an uphill battle. When I was invited to perform at ceremonies in Washington, D.C., honoring Nobel Prize winners, a past winner caused an uproar, saying Miss America had no place on the stage with these esteemed men and women. Fortunately, the current winners discounted his words and welcomed me warmly.

Everywhere I went I reinforced the message, over and over and over again, that Miss America was a role model, a young woman with brains and talent and professional aspirations. Not just a pretty face. Not just a body. I was chipping away at that stereotype, as so many others before me had.

Although I met many famous people as Miss America, I have to say that the most memorable experiences were the everyday encounters—such as the time I was visiting a veterans' hospital and a young man told me, "We've both served America in slightly different ways." That was humbling, and tears came to my eyes when he said it. But I also felt it was true in a deeper sense—that I was an ambassador serving America.

My favorite times were spent with young people. I loved talking to the kids and encouraging them to fulfill their dreams. I knew I could be a role model for them. I saw this early on in Buffalo, New York, when I noticed three *short* girls standing in line for autographs. When I noticed that they had tears in their eyes, I went over to them. "Why are you so sad?" I asked. "We aren't sad," they told me. "We're crying because you've given us hope!" It was true. There was a surge of shorter contestants at the local and state competitions after I won. There were also more violinists. In fact, Rebecca Yeh, Miss Minnesota 2013, who was the fourth runner-up in the Miss America pageant that year, was an accomplished violinist.

One day a little third-grade girl raised her hand and asked, "Why are you so pretty?" The question caught me by surprise, but I went on to talk about the rewards of discovering who you are on the inside, no matter how you looked on the outside.

I also loved meeting young girls who had that spark of pride and confidence I recognized from my own childhood. One day in Dallas a little girl approached me and said, "Hi, Miss America. My name is Heather Carlson."

"Oh, we have the same name," I said with a smile. "Are you by any chance Swedish?"

"No, ma'am," she said fervently. "I'm Texan!"

When David Letterman asked me if Miss America could accept a dinner invitation with a man, I told him I didn't think so. I wasn't really sure. It turned out that there was no rule against Miss America dating—if she could find the time. It had to be arranged on my off days.

The last thing I expected in my jam-packed schedule was that I would meet someone I'd be interested in dating, but that's what happened. Stranger still, Bill turned out to be one of the celebrity judges in the competition. I didn't remember him from that night, but some months later I was asked to speak at a corporate event for his company. We sat next to each other at lunch, and he was very charming. I spoke before he did—thirty minutes onstage with no notes to a roomful of executives. When he got up to speak, he said, "Well, that's a pretty hard act to follow. *I* have notes." I wrote in my diary, going back on the flight, "I like this guy."

We began to see each other occasionally. Bill was forty-five, and at least in my mother's eyes he was too old for me. But my life experience had made me much older than my years. I appreciated being with someone who was mature and successful and whose view of the world was already fully evolved. His connections were nice too. When he invited me to accompany him to George H. W. Bush's inauguration, I was thrilled when the pageant told me I could go.

My friends didn't approve of my dating a man so much older than me, and my mother was beside herself. When I performed with the Greater Twin Cities Youth Symphonies at the Ordway in Saint Paul, Bill flew up to see me play, and we went out to dinner at the Saint Paul Hotel with my family. My mother barely spoke for the entire meal. Bill was nearly her age! She was furious.

During the month that Mom was my companion, I went to see Bill on one of my days off, and there was quite a dustup. She complained to my dad, and he called me, quite upset. "How could you do this to your mother?" he demanded. "You know she doesn't want you to be with him." Yes, I knew, but I realized that it was my life and my choice. She was afraid I would throw away my future life dreams to settle down with someone who had already seen many of his dreams achieved. My mother's opinion meant the world to me, but like every young woman, I needed to establish my independence.

Once when I was in a hotel in Ohio, Bill flew into town to see me. Ellie had her radar out. Somehow she got wind of the plan and she said to me, "Don't you dare think about sneaking out of your room to go see him after hours." I immediately began strategizing how to get out of the room without her knowing. I stuffed a pillow under the connecting door, hoping she wouldn't hear the phone ring when Bill called from the lobby. This was before cell phones and texting, so there was no way to cover up the sound of a ringing phone. When he called, I whispered that I'd be right down and started sneaking out the door, as quietly as I could. Ellie's voice broke the silence. "Gretchen, I know what you're doing." Rats. I had to call him and tell him I couldn't see him. We ended up talking on the phone for hours.

For me, dating Bill made perfect sense. I may have been twenty-two chronologically, but since an early age I'd always been forced to be much more mature than my age, and now the ante was upped further. As Miss America, I wasn't hanging out with twenty-two-year-olds. I was constantly in the company of business and organizational executives. The settings were very worldly, and they required maturity. Those older people, including Bill, seemed to get me in ways that my peers could not, and I was comfortable in their company. It was like being back in the music world, where my experiences were more "adult" than those of my peers. For me it was a great release to feel understood.

My friends didn't understand. After I graduated from Stanford, Bill took me and my two closest friends from school to Le Bernardin, a very expensive restaurant in New York City. When he pulled out his reading glasses to read the menu, my friends looked at me with wide eyes, as if to say, "This guy is *old!*"

The age difference never bothered me. We were just at different places in our lives. I needed to launch my career, and I knew I couldn't just start out in TV in a big city like Chicago, where he lived. I expected to have to move around from city to city, paying my dues. Bill could offer me the world, but I wanted to make my own success in my own way.

It was a week before the pageant to crown Miss America 1990, and my picture was on the cover of *TV Guide.* I thought that was nice—until I read the headline: "A Beauty of a Mistake: Miss America—Was Last Year's Voting Suspect?" My heart sank. What a lousy note to go out on, but realistically, if the cover had said, "Miss America—A Job Well Done," it wouldn't have sold as many issues. The article, written by Lisa DePaulo, raised the possibility that my win was unfair because the celebrity judges hadn't scored the interview as part of the final points. The worst thing about the article was that it wasn't true.

The interview weighed heavily in getting to the top ten, and each of the top ten came into the finals with a composite score. The celebrity panel of judges also got to see the top ten interviews on tape, so it was definitely a factor. You wouldn't know it to read DePaulo's article, which seemed to be based largely on an interview with an anonymous preliminary judge who was disgruntled by the outcome. This judge said my interview was just so-so, not stunning like, say, Miss Colorado's. Based on this evaluation, DePaulo wrote, "Among the top ten in the interview, she was at the bottom of the list. She was very smart. She was very academically skilled but there were many women who did better. Who had the best score in the interview? Miss Colorado. To make matters worse, Carlson barely had the crown on her head when she was already dubbed the smart Miss America." Later it would occur to me that this perspective sounded an awful lot like the view William Goldman expressed in his book. At the time, I felt embarrassed by this "controversy."

I set it aside, determined to enjoy my final week as Miss America. I was doing a lot of media, including guest hosting for the syndicated lifestyle show *PM Magazine* in Atlantic City with the male host. They were looking for a female cohost and they offered me the job. It seemed to be a great professional opportunity. After a year doing media, I was already seriously considering broadcast journalism as a career. But I wanted to be a news journalist, and in those days there was a big delineation between news and entertainment. You couldn't cross that abyss, no matter what.

Coming off the Miss America experience and all the things I

had been through, I thought that no one would take me seriously if I went the entertainment route, because they'd just say, "She got that job because she was Miss America, not because she worked hard for it."

I told them I was returning to my studies at Stanford, and they sweetened the pot, offering to send me to Stanford during the summer hiatus if I worked for them during the year. I still turned them down. I was a planner, and I had the next year all worked out: three months of continued speaking engagements, two quarters at Stanford to finish my degree, and then I'd be ready to start my career. In the long run, it turned out to be the right decision, because PM Magazine folded in 1991. More important, I advanced my career through hard work, not PR, just as I had always done.

When I wasn't doing the show, I was playing the role of the retiring Miss America at the pageant. My wardrobe was set, thanks to a trip to South Carolina to be fitted by Stephen Yearick for some new gowns. One day I spoke at a luncheon for the contestants, and I could feel the raw nerves in the room. I tried to ease the tension by telling the story of the twelve-minute delay and how I spotted the judges poring over the pictures and shaking their heads *no* when they got to mine. I used the story to tell them never to give up on their hopes and dreams, even when they seemed impossible. I also told them that sometimes we learn the greatest lessons about success through the experience of failure—something I had experienced on many occasions in my life. I spoke to them once again, right before the televised pageant, offering them good luck. That's about as close as I got to the contestants. There was no chatting and chumminess because I couldn't show any favoritism.

My happiest moment at the pageant wasn't when I did my farewell walk down the runway. It was when I played my violin for the evening gown portion of the pageant. I wore a black beaded gown with a sweetheart neckline and cap sleeves of black fur (which I later purchased and still have), and played Whitney Houston's song "One Moment in Time." I played with all the passion and feeling in my heart, the words of the song resonating in my mind. It had indeed been a year of "racing with destiny."

The 1990 Miss America, Miss Missouri, Debbye Lynn Turner, was the third African American to win the title. We have remained friends after all these years, as we both worked at CBS News, just two offices away from each other. What are the chances?

After I pinned the crown on Debbye's head, I stepped to the back of the stage. All eyes were on Debbye. I was the past. I recalled a story told by Dorothy Benham, the 1977 Miss America, who was also from Minnesota. She described packing up her things and walking out without fanfare, only to have a little boy spot her and cry out, "Hey, there goes the *old* one." The story made me laugh, because that was exactly how it felt. I took off the makeup and stashed the crown, and now I was just another young woman out in the world. It's almost dizzying how fast the fame goes away— like a stage that turns dark at the end of a performance.

At the same time, I was conscious of striking while the iron was hot—using my platform and contacts to get in the door. That's what I meant when at the end of my Miss America farewell speech onstage I'd said, "This isn't goodbye. This is hello to new beginnings." During my whole year as Miss America and afterward I was calling agents, looking for advice and opportunities. When I was in New York or in Los Angeles doing different appearances, if I had time on my schedule, I tried to meet with executives.

Although I recognize that I had a great advantage in being Miss America, it was still difficult for me to marshal the courage to set up those meetings. For that reason, considering how much nerve it took to pick up the phone, I always tell young people that if they want to get their foot in the door, they should make those calls. You never know what will come of it, and even if you're just starting out, you might encounter interest where you didn't expect it.

I also called people I had met as Miss America—like Deborah Norville, who was so generous with her time. When you're just starting out, you think people like Deborah are too important to talk to you, but I say go for it. You'd be surprised. I think about it today—how much it means to a young person to have a successful person reach out and lend a hand or offer advice. But you have to realize that those people aren't going to come looking for you. You have to take the first step. To this day I have an open door policy. I seek out interns and young women and try to help them. Women mentors were important to me, and I want to do that for others. I'm thrilled when I am able to give someone an early boost in her career. When my intern at *Fox & Friends* got a TV job in Nebraska and wrote to thank me for fighting for her and being a great influence on her, I felt an enormous sense of happiness for her.

Before Miss America, it had been my plan to go to law school after college. That was still in the background—and my LSAT scores were good for five years. But after a year in the spotlight, in front of the public every day, I realized that's where I wanted to be. Broadcast journalism seemed a perfect fit for my personality—fast-paced, driven, never boring, with daily opportunities to shine. I guess you could say that I was led in that direction not just because of my experiences as Miss America, but also because of all those years playing the violin and developing presence on the stage. When I was playing, I was always conscious that people had come to hear me because they wanted to get something out of the experience. The same was true of broadcasting. You had to bring something special to the screen—whether it was breaking news, the emotional connection of a tragedy, or the shared exhilaration of a happy event. I imagined being able to pull news viewers into the moment—to give them something to feel and to think about. I knew I could eventually be good at it. I also knew it would be hard, and I was willing to start at the bottom.

In the months before I returned to Stanford, I kept up the pace of meeting people, hoping that having been Miss America would open doors for me after I graduated from college. I wasn't prepared for the environment I encountered trying to break into television news. In the world of music, where I spent my formative years, we were judged solely on our talent, and gender wasn't a factor. It had never occurred to me, because I hadn't experienced it, that there were people who thought women weren't equal to men in the workplace—much less that some men would try to take advantage of me.

Early on I went to New York to meet with a top television executive I was told could help me. He spent a lot of time with me that day. He called a bunch of shows for me while I was sitting in the office and said, "I'm here with this great young girl. You got to take a look at her. She has a lot of talent." He smiled at me across the desk, and I smiled back, thinking how lucky I was to have such a powerful advocate. Later, he took me out to dinner, where he started imparting "valuable" career advice, including the suggestion that I change my name to "Kristin" for TV. I thought that was strange. Not only is Kristin my sister's name, but I was already pretty well known as Gretchen.

Afterward we got into his car and he gave the driver the address of the friend I was staying with. We were sitting in the backseat together when suddenly he threw himself on top of me and stuck his tongue down my throat. He was all over me, and I can still feel his mouth on my mouth. It makes me a little sick even now. I pulled away from him, desperate to get away. Luckily, we were close to where I was being dropped off. I jumped out of the car and slammed the door without a word, racing into my friend's apartment building. When I got upstairs I broke down and sobbed to my friend Chele. Why would he do that? I thought he respected me. I thought he truly wanted to help me. I was so confused about who I was and what I would face as I moved forward in what appeared to be a really scary world.

How could this happen?

But it did happen—and not only that night in New York. A few months later I was in Los Angeles meeting with a top public relations executive about how to parlay my Miss America experience into a news media career. He suggested we get some dinner. As I got into the passenger seat of his car, he suddenly put his hand on the back of my head and shoved my face into his crotch. Sickened, I yanked myself up and sat frozen, not knowing what to do. This was a very powerful man, and I felt powerless. Somehow I got through the dinner—I'm embarrassed to say I didn't flee, although in that unfamiliar setting I'm not sure where I would have gone. But I spent sleepless nights wondering what I should do next.

Should I tell someone? I thought of the innocent young women who would be crossing these high-profile predators' paths, and it upset me. But whom could I tell? Who would believe me? In my heart I knew that such a he-said, she-said scenario would never favor me. These men were just too powerful. I imagined myself being characterized as a tease, a liar, and worse, and I was frozen with terror. I'm not proud of it, but I stayed silent.

It might seem like a minor event in the retelling, but it had a lasting effect, almost like post-traumatic stress. Many years later, when I was well established, working at Fox News, I saw the PR executive walk past my office door, and I was immediately transported back to that car with my face in his crotch. When he'd gone by, I waited a minute and then jumped up and shut the door so he wouldn't see me. When it was time to leave, I peeked out in the hall to be sure the coast was clear and then ran for the elevator.

Looking back, I see that although these executives might have been genuinely trying to get me a job, they expected something in return. I'd never experienced that before. It was a very uncomfortable wake-up call, but I put these incidents behind me. I knew this sort of thing happened to women, but I wasn't about to let it destroy my confidence or darken my perspective of the world. Two guys who were jerks—I could handle that. But how many other women had this happened to? And if we all said nothing, what does that mean? Have times changed for women? I hope so, but I'm not sure.

During those months I was still booked for a number of appearances, now as the former Miss America. I didn't mind, figuring that the exposure would be positive. At one of the most memorable appearances, I ended up with my hair on fire! *Good Morning*

America had booked me for December 13, which was Santa Lucia Day. In my Swedish heritage, this day involves a very special tradition in which a young woman representing Saint Lucia wears a crown of lit candles during a ceremony. It's very beautiful, and we used to do it as kids at our grandparents' Christmas tea, with either Kris or me playing the role of Saint Lucia. One of us would wear the crown and a white robe with a red sash and walk slowly down the stairs in the house while the others sang the hymn "Santa Lucia." The Swedish Institute pitched *Good Morning America* to show the ceremony, with me as Saint Lucia and a choir of young girls, dubbed the Lucia Maidens, singing.

I was game. Now, that's a lot of fire to carry on your head, and when we did it as kids we always put a wet cloth underneath in case any wax dripped. I guess they skipped the wet cloth on *Good Morning America,* because as I reverently walked down the steps on live TV, a smile pasted on my face and the girls singing behind me, I felt a burning sensation and thought, "My hair is on fire!" I made it through the segment without screaming, but when they took off the crown my hair was clotted with huge clumps of hot wax. They sent me to Vincent, and he sat there with peanut butter and oil, trying to remove the wax. He ended up having to cut off chunks of my hair when he couldn't get all the wax out. It was a close call, and I could only think, "The things we do to get our foot in the door!"

I was glad when it was time to return to Stanford. I was proud to have won the $30,000 scholarship money and was able to pay my way for the remaining time there. My parents were going to have four kids in college, and it meant the world to me that I could help out, thanks to Miss America.

By that point I welcomed a period of anonymity. I lived in an apartment by myself off campus. I didn't really know anybody, because my classmates were long gone by the time I returned. I still remember my first day back, walking across campus wearing jeans, a T-shirt, and tennis shoes—with no makeup. It was liberating, and I felt exhilarated—excited to be back to my studies, back to being normal. I hit the books with new fervor, eager to graduate and get started on my career.

One of the first classes I signed up for—to broaden my horizons—was one in feminist studies. I'm sure my classmates, had they known who I was, would have been surprised to find a recent Miss America in their midst. For me, it was a cathartic experience, a way to decompress after a year when I'd sometimes struggled to be myself in spite of an avalanche of expectations and stereotypes. Even the professor didn't know who I was—until I handed in a paper about being Miss America. My paper contained some deep emotional truths about my experience and the perceptions many people had—especially their high expectations and the tendency to objectify Miss America. I got an A on the paper, but amazingly I don't recall the professor ever saying anything to me about what I'd written. So I remained anonymous.

When I graduated (with honors), I began making the rounds to television stations in Minnesota. One of the first places I went was KSTP in Minneapolis, the local ABC affiliate. I thought I had an inside track there. After I was Miss America, and before I returned to Stanford, I'd been hired as a freelance contributor doing neighborhood stories. I also had the great opportunity to fill in on the show *Good Company*, which was hosted by the husband-and-wife team Sharon Anderson and Steve Edelman. Everyone said I did well, so I hoped I might get a job there. It made perfect sense to me as a launching point.

I had a strong pitch for why I would be an asset to the station. I walked in and gave my pitch to the news director, and he turned me down flat. "Sorry," he said. "You don't have the experience." I thought my time on *Good Company,* my experience as Miss America, and especially being a hometown girl would help me get a job, but the truth of the matter was, I didn't really have a lot of TV know-how for a top-twenty market. And life experience didn't necessarily translate to TV proficiency.

That crushing response is one that college graduates are very used to hearing. It's the impossible conundrum: You can't get hired without experience, and you can't get experience without being hired. The thing is, by then I thought I had a pretty strong portfolio for a twenty-three-year-old.

I went home that night feeling lost and completely blindsided. I sobbed all night in my bed. It was a rude awakening. Being a celebrity didn't mean anything in the real world. Later, even with a long career under my belt, I realized when looking back that nothing in TV ever came easily for me. I've fought for every opportunity, and I've never received that golden call from out of nowhere that changed everything. I accept that now, and it makes me work all the harder, but as a young woman starting out I was shaken by how difficult it was. I thought, "If I can't get a job in my hometown market, where everyone knows me, what hope is there for my career?" I felt discouraged, realizing that once again I was starting at the bottom rung of the ladder and it would be a long climb.

Once I picked myself up and dusted off my hurt ego, I kept plugging away, trying to present a polished, professional persona. One after the other, the local stations turned me down. Then Jody Lomenzo, who had helped me write speeches as Miss America, worked with me to put together a tape of some of my interviews, my *PM Magazine* anchoring, my *Good Company* segments, and even my *Bloopers* tape. I had no idea how to go out and find a TV job in the real world, but Jody lived in Virginia, and one day she called to tell me she'd heard that a reporter job was open at a station in Richmond.

That's when I encountered Wayne Lynch, the news director for WRIC-TV in Richmond, Virginia, who told me he probably wouldn't hire me because I was a former Miss America. I took it as a challenge. Richmond was a long way from home, but by then I was used to making sacrifices to achieve a goal, and I was determined to get my foot in the door wherever that might be. I sent my tape by Federal Express. I hoped Wayne Lynch could see through my inexperience—and his bias about my being Miss America—and spot my potential.

After he got my tape and watched it, Wayne called me a few days later and his tone had changed. Now he said he was interested in hiring me, and he asked me to come and see him in Richmond. In spite of Wayne's initial reluctance, I always felt grateful to him for giving me my start in journalism. He saw my potential, and I was determined to prove him right.

At last, a job!

CHAPTER 6

The Work I Love

My first job in television started with me peeing in a cup.

I flew to Richmond to meet Wayne, and he picked me up at my hotel early in the morning to take me to breakfast. After we had driven for a while, Wayne suddenly pulled up in front of a medical lab and stopped the car.

"What are we doing?" I asked uneasily.

He looked a little chagrined. "Yeah, well, we're going to breakfast. But first you have to go into the lab and take a drug test. They make you urinate into a cup." Wayne kept his eyes straight ahead, but I detected a faint blush creeping over his face.

"What?" I was shocked. All I could think was, "It's seven o'clock in the morning!" But I was a trouper. I sighed, jumped out of the car, and went into the lab. It was the first—and last—time I was ever drug tested. I returned to the car and we went to breakfast.

I guess I passed the drug test, because I was hired for a two-year contract for the princely sum of $18,000 the first year, with a raise to $20,000 in the second. Wayne took me on a tour of the station, and I was very impressed because they had just built a whole studio in the suburbs of Richmond. Everything was very modern and state of the art. I was aware that people were sizing me up as I walked around with Wayne. They knew I'd been Miss America, and I figured some of them were wondering if I was a blonde bimbo. Wayne was still defensive about my past. Asked by a local newspaper if he'd hired me because I was Miss America, he said, "I hired her as a reporter. We're really trying to stay out of the Miss America business here." I had that in mind when I cut my hair to an inch long all the way around shortly after I started the job. It looked awful, and I didn't intend for it to be so short! But I was trying to start fresh on my new adventure.

My first job was to report for "Neighborhood News," a twice-weekly feature on the local community. It was mostly good news reporting, showing all the wonderful people who were doing things that mattered. The fact is, viewers love hearing good news. They get tired of the fires and murders and robberies.

Writing scripts in 1990 could be an arduous process, because we were still using typewriters and carbon paper. There was the top sheet, white, then the black carbon sheet, then a pink sheet, a blue sheet, and a yellow sheet. The production assistants sat at long tables and ripped scripts. If you made even one mistake, the whole thing would have to be done over, or you could laboriously use Wite-Out on each copy. The old technology added hours to an already full schedule. We were relieved when we got computers in 1991.

In my first months at WRIC I lived in a small one-bedroom apartment. My furniture consisted of a futon I'd had in college, a stair climber, and a table and chairs. It wasn't exactly nesting. I came home every night dead tired, ordered pizza, and plugged my TV into the single wall outlet. There were no ceiling lights, so until I got a lamp I ate by the light of the bathroom and TV. I didn't know anybody, and it was a bare-bones existence, but my work consumed me.

I was like every other young woman beginning a career. I poured everything into my work, just as I had always done. The discipline I learned as a girl was now turned toward my job, and it was all I thought about.

Looking back to our early careers, we don't always recall that intense feeling of fear and anticipation that goes with being green. You step into an unfamiliar world. Every moment is loaded with meaning. Every decision seems do-or-die—especially if you're in an intensely competitive field like broadcasting. I was always aware that I had to prove myself every day, and I figured that if I couldn't be the most seasoned journalist, I'd be the hardest working.

In short order I graduated to the crime beat. I got out and started visiting crime scenes and cold-calling for comments. I faced daily rejection. When you're trying to get people to talk to you, nine out of ten say no. It was a high-stress business, because I was always conscious of needing to get the story. The pervasive thought in my head was, "If I lose this story I'm dead."

People on the phone seemed to have a very hard time getting my name straight, which tickled me. In Minnesota, Carlson is a very common name—it's the fattest section in the phone book. Suddenly my name was unfamiliar. When I called and left messages in Richmond, most often the people on the phone would say, "Gretchen what? *Carlton?*" I got a kick out of that. I stood out.

I was on the beat every day, racing around the city, and I quickly overcame my lifetime problem with carsickness. I'd be bouncing along in a speeding car, usually with a cameraman at the wheel, writing scripts on a notepad, and there just wasn't time for throwing up. I practiced mind over matter, and eventually it took. Some of the cameramen smoked, and occasionally I'd bum a cigarette to settle my nerves.

A significant amount of my time was spent covering executions, because they had a lot of executions in Virginia. I did interviews with the people who were going to be put to death, and it made an indelible impression on me. I can remember peering through the glass partition as I interviewed men (it was always men during my time reporting) who were scheduled to die. One of my memorable interviews was with Roger Keith Coleman, a coal miner who was on death row after being convicted of the rape and murder of his sister-in-law. He never stopped proclaiming his innocence, and he had a huge support network. Governor Douglas Wilder received thousands of letters in favor of clemency, which he denied. Coleman even made the cover of *Time* magazine, with the headline "This Man Might Be Innocent." I spoke to him the day of his scheduled execution, while he was awaiting word from the Supreme Court. That morning he had taken a lie detector test in a last-ditch effort to clear his name. He told me, "I will fight to prove I'm innocent until I'm either free or dead." He failed the lie detector test and the Supreme Court refused to issue a stay. Hours later he was dead. Many people continued to believe in Coleman's innocence, but a decade later, DNA tests on semen from the rape confirmed his guilt.

When I interviewed the prisoners, it was usually about the appeals process and what they were doing to try to stay their executions. The lawyers were always angling to get a lot of press, but I would also talk to the families of the victims, and their stories often moved me to tears. It was an emotional roller coaster. I felt the grief of the families, yet, sitting behind that glass partition, I would think, "I'm looking at a man who will be dead in a week." Or sometimes the very next day.

I never personally witnessed an execution, although I put my name on the list and wanted to. But I did everything else. I was allowed to get video of the execution cell, which was located close to the death chamber. One time I went in to get shots of the electric chair, which they called Old Sparky, and they were conducting a dress rehearsal for an execution. The sound of the chair revving up was chilling. Minutes later, as I was sitting at the glass partition interviewing the man who would be executed the next day, he asked, "What's that noise?" I winced at the question, but replied honestly, "It's the chair."

In twenty-four hours I was doing a live shot outside the penitentiary, reporting that he was dead, and "for his last meal he requested pizza and chocolate-covered strawberries."

A lot of my reporting time was spent on the streets of Richmond, where there was an escalating crime wave during that period. It got to the point where we usually didn't cover murders unless three or more people died.

I used to send my mom tapes, and I'd wait anxiously to hear her review. She'd watch them and call me. "You know honey," she'd say, "it would be just great if you could smile a little more. I'd like the world to see your personality, because you're funny and you have such a pretty smile."

"Mom," I'd protest, "I'm covering murders. I can't say three people died with a big smile on my face."

She'd sigh. "I just want people to know who you are, because I don't feel like they're seeing who you really are deep down."

I couldn't fight her charm offensive. I just said, "Mom, that's why I'm killing myself, so that one day I can get a morning show where I can be personable. You can come on during the cooking segment and show me how to do it." I was teasing her, but I thought if she really knew what I was doing in Richmond every day, she'd have a coronary.

The danger I faced didn't always come from the streets. Sometimes it was on the inside. One day I went out with a cameraman I didn't know very well to cover a story in a rural area, quite a distance from the city. Before the interview, he helped me attach my microphone, reaching up under my blouse to clip it to my bra. This was a normal thing. I didn't think anything of it.

We did the interview, and then we got back into the car for the long ride back to the station. I was relaxing against the headrest, thinking about the story, when he spoke.

"How did you like it when I put that microphone under your shirt?" he asked. "I was touching your breasts as I was putting the microphone on."

I sat up straight, thinking, "Oh, God." Suddenly I was terrified. We were in the middle of nowhere and I was in the car with a lunatic. For a moment I actually thought about opening the door and rolling out of the car, like you see in the movies. I wondered how much it would hurt.

He kept talking in a low, seductive voice about my breasts and his feelings, and I was seriously frightened. I didn't know what he was going to do. I'd been harassed before, of course, but this was different. It was ominous and scary. When we stopped for gas, I thought about calling the station, thinking it might be a matter of life and death. This was before cell phones. But I got my panic under control and decided against it. I was very conscious of being new to the job and not wanting to be pegged as a troublemaker or a hysteric. I held my emotions in check and continued the painfully long drive back to the station, pressed against the passenger-side door as far as I could physically get from him.

By the time we got there I was a basket case. I was pale and shaking. The assistant news director immediately saw that something was wrong with me. He pulled me into his office and asked, "What's wrong with you? What happened?" I said, "Nothing. I'm fine." I wasn't, of course. I was terrified. Terrified I would not be believed if I said anything. Terrified that I had joined a profession of predators. Terrified that I would jeopardize my career if I ratted out my harasser.

But my boss, God bless him, kept pressing me. I really didn't want to talk about it, but he was extremely intent on making sure I told him what was wrong. I finally caved. It turned out there were other issues with the photographer, and the station let him go. Like so many young women who are the victims of harassment, I worried for months that I had invited his advances in some way—that I had done something wrong, which was not the case.

In the years since, I have always felt great compassion for women who are caught in the vise of a sexual harassment scandal. Even though we have laws against it and HR departments to handle it, a woman—especially if she is young and just starting out—can never be sure that reporting harassment won't hurt her career. Had my boss not pressed me to talk about what happened to me, I probably would have said nothing and been alone with my misery and shame. And even then I was worried that people would find out and blame me. I cling to the hope that with more and more women in the workplace, we can teach younger generations to be respectful, and also encourage young women to speak up when they've experienced abuse. One positive sign is that many companies provide sexual harassment training to their employees. Mine does. Nobody particularly enjoys going to those training sessions, but they are an important demonstration that the issue is being taken seriously in the corporate world. And, of course, it's not just women who attend those sessions. Men are a big part of the process. It shouldn't be solely up to the woman to figure out how to deal with being harassed.

I believe that the harassment problem will continue to dissipate as a younger generation of men comes into the workforce. I understand this in a personal way. One of the main reasons I feel it is so important for me to have a career is not only to be a good role model for my daughter, but also for my son. Part of putting an end to harassment involves educating boys to be completely accepting of women in the workplace so that they grow into men who model that respect.

We talk a lot about creating opportunity for women. I believe this conversation is 50 percent about men. It's not only about women having the confidence to stand up, raise their hands, and sit in the front row, but also about men's perceptions about women's capabilities. And that starts when they're young boys.

Less than a year after I started at the station, Wayne left to join a regional cable start-up, and he was replaced by a woman named

Joyce Reed, who became my first mentor in the news business. There weren't a lot of women news directors then, but Joyce was a powerhouse. Before coming to Richmond she had been a news director for stations in El Paso, Kansas City, and Springfield, Missouri. Joyce had great physical presence. She was tall and slender, with long curly hair and a strong personality. She was a career woman through and through, divorced with no children. And she had a reputation for being "tough." A lot of the men in management positions at the station were nervous. There was a whispering campaign that she might fire all the men, which seemed a little silly, but paranoia was high.

I was excited about Joyce coming in as news director. Tough didn't scare me. I always liked having a boss who actually paid attention to detail and had high expectations. And she quickly saw how hard I was working and handed me a great opportunity. One day she called me in and announced, "You're going to be the political reporter now, covering the governor every day." I was thrilled but scared. The guy who'd been handling the political beat had been doing it for twenty-five years. His Rolodex was a mile long. I would be starting from scratch and I'd have to hit the ground running. Truth be told, most of the political reporters in our state were older white men, so there was extra pressure.

Maybe Joyce recognized that experience wasn't the only value—that there was something to be said for sending out someone young and hungry. Maybe she was trying to create more of an edge. Whatever her reasons, I was grateful for the opportunity, and I loved political reporting. But it was hard work because I was under the gun to prove myself and not make too many mistakes.

At first lawmakers would regularly refer to me as "honey" and "sweetie." I would politely correct them, saying my name was Gretchen. Eventually they got it. I guess we were learning together— me how to be a political reporter, and them how to work with a woman in what was typically a man's role.

In this position I discovered my love of political and investigative reporting. I saw that I would have a chance to dig beneath the surface and discover information no one else knew—to be first with the scoop. It was a rush.

Without a doubt the biggest political story I covered was a scandal involving Governor Douglas Wilder and Senator Chuck Robb, both of them men with higher political ambitions. It was no secret that Wilder was angling to challenge Robb in the 1994 Senate primary, and the two had an ongoing feud. The ensuing scandal landed in my lap early in my time as a political reporter, when three of Robb's top aides were fired for allegedly recording Wilder's phone conversations. A grand jury was empaneled, and every reporter in Virginia, including me, was on the story, trying to get to the bottom of the wiretapping question. As I followed the case, it was more for me than just wanting a scoop that would elevate my position. I found that I loved the investigative process of trying to solve a mystery. It consumed every waking moment. I was cultivating sources in the district attorney's office and with the FBI, and at one point it looked like it was all going to come together when a guy straight out of the "Deep Throat" playbook contacted me and said he was connected to the person who knew the truth. Not only that, but he was willing to be fitted with a microphone and have a conversation with the source. It was high drama! We met him at a mall in the Richmond suburbs and wired him with all our fancy equipment, and off he went. And we never saw him again. He stole our microphone! One minute I thought I was going to break the case wide open, and the next minute I was left with a red face. In the end, nothing came of the story and it faded from the news.

Joyce never gave me a hard time about my failure, assuring me that these things happened. I know she saw that special passion in me that makes a good reporter. She trusted me to do a good job and she raised my cachet in the newsroom, especially among those who were suspicious about having a former Miss America in their midst. I always pitched stories at the morning meeting, because pitching stories is the bread and butter of reporting. Joyce would say, "Everyone should be pitching stories like Gretchen." She helped me build a reputation for seriousness. But I also learned some important lessons about succeeding as a woman. Working hard and being smart were not enough. I had to call on other qualities, like humility and compassion and talking about *we,* not *I.* Maybe men don't feel that same pressure, but for women these qualities are like a secret weapon.

As I gained more experience, Joyce started tapping me to fill in as an anchor, mostly on the early morning newscast. I was literally a one-woman show—the scriptwriter, the producer, and the anchor. I had to be at the station at 2:30 in the morning. I drove there and let myself into the empty newsroom, where I finalized my scripts for the show and then did my own hair and makeup.

On air, while delivering the news, I had to run my own teleprompter with my hand. I also timed the broadcast to do the local news cut-ins during the breaks from ABC News and *Good Morning America.* Thinking back on it, I almost can't believe that they left everything up to a twenty-three-year-old without having an executive producer on hand. I was terrified most of the time, but I got through it without making any noticeable mistakes.

After I survived the broadcast, I breathed a sigh of relief, went to McDonald's, and ordered a big breakfast of pancakes, eggs, and sausage. Then I went home and slept.

Being in charge of the early morning newscast allowed me to stretch myself to do something outside my comfort zone. Looking back, I see that having big challenges early in your career stays with you so that every time you come up against a new challenge you can pull up the memory and say, "If I could do *that,* I can do *this.*"

The fame I achieved as Miss America seemed long past. Now I was striving to make my way in the world. But one man never let go of the image of me as Miss America, and he began a reign of terror that would last for years.

One day Constantine Kargas showed up at my parents' house in Anoka. He was a big man, carrying a large black garbage bag with his possessions. My mother and a cleaning lady were alone in the house that day. When Mom answered the door to find this large stranger on the porch, she was polite. "Yes, may I help you?"

He identified himself and said, "I'm here to pick up your daughter Gretchen." As Mom gaped at him, he explained that we were leaving together to get married. Mom's first thought was that she had to call Dad. She asked Kargas to wait and closed the door. Then she called Dad at Main Motors, and he called the police before he rushed home. Mom stayed inside and waited, and she was nervous. She didn't know if he had a gun. The cleaning lady locked herself in the bathroom. Dad arrived shortly, and he was standing outside the front door with Kargas when the police car arrived. The officers gave Kargas a warning to cease contact and sent him home to Wisconsin on a bus. Since he had no money, my dad even paid for his bus ticket.

I thought he was one of those weird Miss America superfans, and I didn't think too much about it until I started receiving letters from him at the station. He wrote about how much he loved me and how we were destined to be together. He wrote that he had everything planned for our life together. The letters were not threatening, but they were creepy. Their tone was overly familiar— as if we had an ongoing relationship where I had professed my love to him too. Now his appearance on my parents' doorstep took on an ominous cast. One day I happened to notice that the postmark on a letter sent to me at the TV station was Richmond. I felt pure terror. How long would it be until he found out where I lived?

Around that time my mother visited me, and while we were walking down the street she was mugged and punched by a bunch of teenagers who stole her purse. That was horrifying enough, but when we got back to the apartment I suddenly realized that she had my key in her purse, and it was marked with the name of the apartment complex and my apartment number. I had to move the next day.

Several months after my mother's mugging, the Richmond police called with a frightening story. Kargas had been walking down the street in Richmond when he was mugged. In a videotaped interview the police asked him, "Why are you in Richmond?" He said, "I'm here to pick up my friend Gretchen Carlson. We're going away together." He told the police that he had moved to Richmond to be near me.

The police brought the videotape to my apartment, and we sat on the couch and watched it. I was shaking as I saw Kargas's face and heard him speak for the first time. This was my stalker, and I felt the madness in his calm insistence that we were a couple.

"What can I do?" I asked the police officers, desperate to find a quick resolution. Unfortunately, there wouldn't be one. The officers explained that since Kargas hadn't threatened me, there was not much they could do. They gave me a printout of his face from the video, which the station posted at the security desk. There was little chance he could get to me at work. But what about the rest of my life?

From then on, every time I received a letter, I looked for a threat, hoping he'd cross a line so we could bust him. But he was smart enough or lucky enough to avoid any language that could be construed as menacing, even though the very nature of his contact was a menace. I had dark visions not just of being killed, but of being kidnapped and whisked away to another destination.

It's hard to fully describe the constant fear and sense of helplessness that comes with having a stalker. Every time I received a letter, a paralyzing dread overcame me. It may have been the cost of being in the public eye, but I wondered if the cost would be my life. I was well aware of the story of the actress Rebecca Schaeffer, who was murdered by her stalker in 1989. Robert John Bardo had been stalking Schaeffer for years before he showed up at her door with a gun and shot her in the chest. This story of obsessive love eventually turned into one of obsessive hate, the common pattern of stalkers. After the murder, there was a lot of talk about how it could have been prevented—how Schaeffer might have been protected. But as I found out, there is no easy protection from stalkers.

Until someone actually commits a crime, the police can't take any action.

I went home for a visit, and Dad wasn't taking the threat too seriously. Mom said to him, "Do you want your daughter to end up in a box?" I'll never forget her saying that. We all looked at each other in shock. This was deadly real.

I was outraged that there was virtually nothing that could be done to stop Kargas. This was a man I'd never met, had never spoken to, had never encouraged in any way, yet he had insinuated himself into my everyday life. Did I have to be kidnapped or killed for anyone to take action? Could I ever again feel safe? Kargas was clearly mentally ill, but that was no comfort to me. My dad even reached out to his family. His mother said he had been in medical school at Duke when he began his downward spiral. She cried on the phone, "I can't control him when he doesn't take his medicine." Great!

For a time my parents considered hiring full-time security guards for my apartment in Richmond. But then I received a good job offer from WCPO, the CBS affiliate in Cincinnati, and I moved. It was a great professional opportunity, but I also thought I might escape from my stalker by moving to another city. I was heartsick when I received the first love letter from Kargas shortly after joining WCPO. There would be no escape. In fact, Kargas was obviously getting impatient for us to start our life together. In one letter he announced that our wedding date was scheduled for June 30, 1994, and we would be traveling to Greece for our honeymoon. One day a dozen roses and a box of candy arrived for me at work, and the florist verified that the sender was Kargas. He wasn't even trying to hide his name. He later called Cincinnati Bell and tried to get my home phone number.

At this point, law enforcement was taking notice. In Cincinnati, while doing news stories, I became friendly with a prosecutor in the DA's office, and he was more proactive. He gave me an alarm I could wear around my neck that would call 911 if I pressed it. It was hooked up to my phone and it only worked if I was within one hundred yards of my apartment. The idea was that if I got out of my car and he was there, I could press the alarm and the police would know it was him. But what if he was there with a gun? What if he grabbed me and put me in a car? The alarm was better than nothing, but it didn't make me feel safe.

I also had help from a neighbor, a lawyer who became a good friend and spent many nights sleeping on my floor with a poker at hand. That's how scared I was. The last straw was when I received a diamond engagement ring at work. It had been purchased at a jeweler in Madison, Wisconsin.

Finally, after years of harassment, there was enough evidence to bring a criminal case against Kargas on the grounds of "menacing by stalking," and a temporary restraining order was signed forbidding him from having any contact with me, my parents, or the Miss America pageant. I didn't believe a restraining order would have much effect on a mentally ill man who was so convinced that we had a relationship. Indeed, he did violate the restraining order, continuing to send me letters until his arrest.

Kargas's trial date was set in Madison, and the prosecutor asked me to fly out and testify. Needless to say, the last thing I wanted was to be in a courtroom only a few feet away from the man who had terrorized me. I couldn't stomach the idea that he would see me face-to-face and become more obsessed. I didn't want him to have the power to bring me into a room with him. I hired a lawyer in Madison to submit a motion to the court approving telephone testimony, and I was relieved when it was granted. I wouldn't have to see him.

I remember the day of my testimony as if it were yesterday. I sat in a room at the Cincinnati Police Department with Bill Fletcher, my detective on the case, who had been by my side throughout the whole ordeal. I had lived in fear for years, and I was so grateful to this man who had believed in me and helped me. I was shaking like a leaf as I listened to Kargas speak. Although he was hundreds of miles away, the sound of his voice terrified me.

I testified for the whole morning, detailing every step of the horrible journey. When I was done, somehow I managed to pull myself together and go to work at two o'clock for my full shift. It's what I had learned in life—that strength came from perseverance and never giving up no matter what the challenge. I decided I would solve this problem too and not back down even though my life was at risk. I had to put on a game face and move on.

The sad truth of stalker cases is that even when they reach the level of the criminal court, the results are rarely satisfying. In 1995 Kargas was convicted on multiple counts of harassment and violating a restraining order, but the bulk of his sentence of three years was reduced to probation. In all he served only seventy days in prison. It seemed like weak justice to me, that a man could create such terror and upheaval in a stranger's life and be so mildly punished. Worse still, I had to go on with my life with the haunting knowledge that he was out there in the world. I never heard from him again, but over the years, as my profile increased, I often thought about him and dreaded the day he might reappear and threaten me or my family. It was like a gnawing ache in the back of my mind—which is just one more way stalkers exert a cruel power over the people they target.

When I contemplated telling this story in the book, I wasn't sure I wanted to stir up that old fear. I was surprised when I learned Kargas had died in 2008. I decided it was important to talk about my experience, because I knew that countless other women were enduring the same threat. Occasionally these incidents are publicized when they involve high-profile people. However, the larger crisis is experienced by millions of people who are not public figures. The National Center for Victims of Crime reports that more than six million stalking incidents were recorded in a one-year period. Although every state now has laws against stalking, there is never complete peace for those of us who have experienced it. Our criminal justice system hasn't even begun to address this problem, and that's why I'm telling my story, hoping to play a small part in a necessary wake-up call.

Being stalked could have put a damper on my experience in Cincinnati, but I didn't let it. I loved working at WCPO. The first piece of advice my news director, Jim Zarchin, gave me was quite profound. He said, "I want you to do live TV like you play the violin." When I asked what he meant, he said, "I've seen you play—the same passion, the feeling you have inside—that's what I want you to do."

I never forgot his words, and they meant a lot to me then. I was already poised to work as hard as I could, but relating my job to my violin and my passion for it gave me another way of looking at my career. I began to see that this inherent drive and spirit could shine through in whatever I was reporting. And one of the best things about WCPO was that it was a powerhouse station with a deep commitment to long-form stories and the money to spend on them. Sometimes I'd be off the streets for a month or so putting together a major report or investigative piece. One that I was especially proud of involved a group of high-risk kids and an organization that worked with them for a year to improve the trajectory of their futures. I was able to follow them through each stage of their progress, and the station led the evening news with my reports—right up to the emotional graduation of these amazing kids who now had a future they'd never expected.

When I wasn't doing long stories, I was a nightside reporter. That's where I really honed my skills on live TV. Broadcasts were at 5:00, 5:30, 6:00, and 11:00, and I spent my time in a live truck. When there was breaking news anywhere in Cincinnati, I went out in the truck. We had little time for editing. The mandate was, "Just get out there and tell us what happened." In the live truck I would cut quick one-minute pieces, record my voice, edit, and feed the whole piece back to the station. Sometimes I just sent my voice tracks back and picked sound bites from people I'd interviewed, and the final piece would be edited at the station. The pressure was constant, and I found that I thrived in that environment.

I lived in a great area called Mount Adams, an enclave on a hill that overlooked the city, and began to enjoy myself, though it took a little time to get settled in. My first Christmas, soon after I arrived, was spent working. I wasn't much of a cook, and I ate a can of beans at my apartment for Christmas dinner—a far cry from the usual festivities back home. I hadn't realized that all the stores would be closed. It wasn't the last holiday I worked, for sure.

Gradually I started to fit in. Many of my colleagues at the station were young and single, and we hung out together. I'd get home from work at 11:45 p.m. and then go out. Some nights I didn't get to bed until 1:00 or 2:00 in the morning.

Bill Hemmer, now my colleague at Fox, was the weekend sports anchor at WCPO, and we became close friends. Bill is a couple of years older than me, and while we were at the station together he did an incredibly daring thing for a young up-and-coming newscaster. He took a leave and traveled the world for a year, not knowing for sure if he'd have a job when he got back. Fortunately, the station knew what it had in Bill. When he began sending video reports from his travels, they aired them on the evening news as an ongoing segment called "Bill's Excellent Adventure," which won him two Emmys. Bill's career only got better once he returned from his travels, and soon he was snapped up by CNN and then Fox. However, what has stuck with me is that he took a risk. He didn't know if it would hurt or help him professionally, but he felt compelled to do it. I admire that quality.

A television coach once analyzed my career and advised me, "You need to learn how to take risks." It was the way I could set myself apart. I wasn't exactly sure what taking risks would mean for me, but the advice caused me to reflect once again about my violin training. I was always told that many people could learn to play the notes, but what distinguished those with a true gift was the ability to stand out by risking a unique interpretation.

The same was true of TV. What fresh interpretation could I risk?

That opportunity came to me when I made my next move to WOIO CBS-19 News in Cleveland, where I became part of a great experiment—two women coanchors for the evening news broadcasts at 6:00 and 11:00. My coanchor, Denise Dufala, was a native of Cleveland, and she was popular with viewers, but the station was suffering from chronically low ratings and the female duo was an attempt to lift them.

I had originally been hired to do the weekend news while Denise and her male coanchor, Steve Coleman, did the evening news. But as ratings faltered, the news director, Kim Godwin, and the station higher-ups had the radical idea of pairing Denise and me in the evenings. They promoted us as "the right team at the right time."

A plaque on my desk read, "A person who risks nothing does nothing, has nothing and is nothing." With that in mind I jumped into this new challenge wholeheartedly. Denise and I complemented each other—and it wasn't just that she was brunette and I was blonde. Our personalities were distinct. Denise had anchoring experience. I was the new kid on the block, a few years younger and much greener. We were scrutinized to death, but Denise laughed at the idea that having women coanchors was at all risky. "The only difference between two females and a male and a female is that we have to coordinate the color of our outfits every day," she joked. That was true—after the unfortunate night when Denise wore orange and I wore pink. We got a call from an executive at the station who complained that it looked as if a pumpkin had exploded in a raspberry field.

CHAPTER 7

Kindred Spirits

My career was going well, but as I approached thirty, I was worried about my personal life. As an evening newscaster I had very little opportunity to socialize, and I hadn't dated anyone for a while. I thought I was in danger of becoming one of those newswomen I'd seen so often who were married to their jobs. Not that I faulted them if that was their choice, which it often was. But it wasn't *my* choice. Feeling sorry for myself, I regularly complained to my mother that I hadn't met the right man. She always replied, "Don't worry, honey. He's right around the corner." She told me, "You just never know. He'll come when you're not looking." I wasn't sure that I believed her.

I had become good friends with my real estate agent, Patti, and her best friend was also a real estate agent who had just sold a house to a "great guy"—a former pro baseball player who was now a baseball agent. His name was Casey Close. They decided to try to fix us up, and we were both agreeable. Casey was going to call me. I said okay and put it out of my mind.

I was on the bus with the Dawgs the first time Casey called me. The Dawgs were a group of rabid Cleveland Browns fans, named for the bleacher section where they sat—the Dawg Pound. Their rowdy behavior, reportedly fueled by alcohol, included wearing dog masks, barking wildly, and throwing Milk-Bones at visiting teams.

The Browns' owner, Art Modell, had just announced plans to relocate the team to Baltimore, and as you can imagine, the announcement was like red meat to the Dawgs. I was covering a trip to a game in Pittsburgh where they were planning a raucous protest.

When my cell phone rang, I was sitting next to Big Dawg, and the bus was rocking with the trademark Dawg chant: *Woof . . . woof . . . woof.*

I answered the phone, shouting to be heard above the uproar.

"Yes," said a friendly voice. "My name is Casey Close. I'm calling you because . . ." He was drowned out by a fresh series of chants: *Woof . . . woof . . . woof.*

Speaking louder, Casey asked, "Where *are* you?"

"I'm on a bus with the Dawgs," I shouted back. "I'm going to Pittsburgh to cover a story."

"Cool!" Now he sounded enthusiastic. "Do you like sports?"

"I love sports," I yelled as the bus heaved with sound and motion.

"When can you go on a date?" he yelled back.

We had our first date a couple of weeks after I returned from Pittsburgh. Casey came to pick me up at my apartment, and I can still see him standing at the security door waiting for me to buzz him in. He was very handsome—tall and athletic, with wavy dark hair—and holding a bouquet of flowers.

I knew next to nothing about him, other than that he was from Ohio and he'd played professional baseball before becoming an agent. He was understated about his achievements, but later when I looked him up I was impressed. In college at the University of Michigan, Casey was a star—in fact, he still holds the career record for home runs. In 1986 he was drafted by the New York Yankees and spent five years in their minor league farm clubs, eventually working his way up to the top tier of Triple A. He then went on to play Triple A with the Seattle Mariners for two years. Now he was a sports agent building a strong clientele.

Casey was driving a Jeep, and he took me to a nice restaurant. We immediately hit it off. It wasn't love at first sight, but we were on the same wavelength. Casey was warm and open and hilariously funny. We were laughing so hard and talking so much that we kept forgetting to look at the menu.

"Oh my gosh," I said. "We really should order, but you are so funny." And then I delivered the biggest diss of his life.

I was looking at him across the table, and I suddenly said, "You remind me so much of somebody famous." He sat back in his chair with a little smile on his face as if he knew exactly what I was going to say, because he'd heard it a million times. I later learned that people often said he resembled John F. Kennedy Jr., and he was expecting me to say just that. But what I said was, "Jim Carrey."

The smile disappeared. His face fell. He looked shocked. I thought, "Oh, crap." I knew I'd put my foot in it and probably ruined everything.

I excused myself and went to the ladies' room, where I took out my cell phone and called Patti.

"I just totally screwed this thing up," I said miserably.

"What are you talking about? Where are you?"

"In the bathroom. I just said he reminded me of the actor Jim Carrey."

"So what?" I know she thought I was demented. I told her his reaction.

"So," she asked, "will you mind if he doesn't call you tomorrow?"

I hurriedly said, "No. It's okay. No big deal."

Was it? I didn't know. But I liked him.

He did call me again, and I was starting to *really* like him. By the third date, our conversation was growing deeper. I realized that here was a guy who just might *get* me. Like me, he was very driven, and he admired that quality in me. We were living parallel lives. Casey had stopped playing baseball, and now he was killing himself to become a successful baseball agent, just as I was killing myself to succeed in the news business. But more than that, our childhoods had parallels. He understood what I went through as a young musician because he went through a similar experience as a baseball player. When I told him about my wrenching decision to quit the violin, he actually understood on a very personal level. He too had faced a similar wrenching decision. Playing Triple A ball was a tough environment of endless bus trips and little income. But most players start there, always with the goal of moving up to the majors. I'm sure Casey visualized himself walking out onto the field at Yankee Stadium, just as I once visualized myself playing at Carnegie Hall.

In spite of his performance as a hitter, by 1991 Casey saw that the window of opportunity for playing in the major leagues was closing and he was faced with a choice. He was twenty-six years old when he decided to quit playing—a very emotional decision for a man who had devoted so many years to the sport. Although he found a way to remain in the baseball profession as a sports agent, I identified with the struggle he went through. I had been there myself. When you are considered a prodigy, whether in sports or music or something else, your identity is shaped by that ability and your worth is measured by how well you do. Both Casey and I were driven, extremely focused people. Choosing to walk away is like falling into a canyon without a net. You have to redefine yourself. I was drawn by the fact that Casey and I had that in common. We understood each other.

I had usually dated older guys, but Casey brought out something different in me. We had similar timelines, a shared willingness to sacrifice, and the same drive. We could talk for hours about our experiences and our dreams. If there is such a thing as a soul mate, I began to see that he might be that for me.

I knew what I wanted in life, though. On our third date I said to Casey, "If you don't want to eventually live in New York City, don't call me back." The underlying message was: "Don't call me back if you don't also want a partner with a fulfilling career." He smiled and said that New York was his dream too.

We hadn't been dating very long when I told Casey I was planning to join my parents in Arizona for a vacation. They had semiretired to Arizona and lived there in the winter, and my mom and dad loved to golf—a sport I didn't love only because I never had time to practice and was worried I wasn't that good. As a kid I told my dad I liked driving the golf cart better than playing! Casey announced that he was going to be in Arizona for spring training and would like to see me and maybe even meet my parents.

Whoa! Was I ready for that? My mom rarely liked the men I dated. I wasn't sure I wanted to subject Casey to that scrutiny, and I was really afraid she wouldn't like him, although if I'd been thinking straight I would have realized that of course she would, and she did. My parents loved Casey. So did my grandfather. When I first told him about Casey he asked, "Is he Swedish?" I said no. "Is he Lutheran?" No again. At last he asked, "Is he a nice guy?" I said yes. He smiled and gave me his blessing.

After visiting my parents, we drove through the desert to Sedona, where we stood at the dramatic site of the Chapel of the Holy Cross, a citadel on a hill, designed by a student of Frank Lloyd Wright. Alone there, we gazed out on the endless hills, taking in the natural beauty. It was very romantic.

Soon after the Arizona trip, we drove to Columbus, Ohio, where I was introduced to Casey's parents. I wore my favorite outfit—a hot little leather jumper that I wore with tights, which was very stylish at the time. They told me that I was the first woman Casey had ever brought to meet them. I wasn't sure whether to believe it, but Casey was grinning and I thought it could be true. That meant something to me.

One evening, ten months into our relationship, Casey showed up on my doorstep with a surprise. He sat down on the couch and rooted around in his pocket, pulling out a ring on a chain. It was his University of Michigan championship ring. He dangled it in front of me and said, "I can't afford a ring right now, but will this do for a commitment?" I melted. I knew it was a pretty big step for him, and it really was a commitment. That ring was important to him! I began wearing it around my neck.

That Christmas we planned to fly to Minnesota to visit my parents and then go to Columbus on Christmas Day to see Casey's parents. Unbeknownst to me, Casey was planning to ask me to marry him while we were in Minnesota. He had ordered the ring, and because of last-minute timing, the jeweler arranged to deliver it to him at the airport. Casey told the jeweler they had to make the transaction with the highest amount of secrecy. "Gretchen is an investigator," he said. "She knows everything. If she sees you, she'll figure it out." They agreed to meet in the men's room outside security.

We got to the airport, and we were running late. Casey said, "I have to go to the bathroom." I was annoyed. "What? Come on, we have to go through security. There's no time."

He was in the bathroom forever, and I was getting pissed. Apparently the two men crowded into a single stall—one stall, four feet. That must have raised a few eyebrows!

Finally, Casey shoved the ring in his bag and came out. But then he was worried that the security officer would see it and make a comment, so he was staring bug-eyed at the guy, like, "Please, keep my secret."

When we got to the gate, Casey said, "I have to go to the bathroom." I stared at him with disbelief. "What are you talking about? You just went to the bathroom." But of course he hadn't.

He kept the ring in his pocket the whole time, so I wouldn't see it. On our first night in Minnesota, he quietly asked my parents for permission to marry their daughter. He told them he was going to ask me the next day. I was completely oblivious to the drama going on around me. My investigative skills were on vacation.

The following day we went to the Mall of America, which was relatively new at the time. We were planning to shop and then meet my sister and her boyfriend at a Minnesota Timberwolves basketball game in downtown Minneapolis. It was a long day and there was a blizzard expected.

I called home at one point to check with my mom about the storm prediction. She was acting very strange, asking me leading questions: "How's your day? Did anything *special* happen?"

"Uh, no, not really. We're just shopping. We ate at the Rainforest Café."

"I hope it's a *fantastic* day for you," she said brightly.

"Okay. See you later." I hung up and joked to Casey, "My mom sure is hyper today."

We drove home that night in a blizzard. The snow was piling up and I just wanted to get there. Then, at the top of the driveway, with snow blowing all around us, Casey stopped the car and pulled the parking brake.

"What are you doing?" I asked. Casey was starting to get on my nerves. Didn't he realize we were in the middle of a blizzard? Then he reached into his pocket and took out the ring. "Gretchen," he said solemnly, as the wind and snow pounded against the car, "you are the woman I want to spend the rest of my life with. Will you marry me?"

I burst into tears, saying, "Yes! Yes!" and trying to hug him across the seats. Finally he said, "Your mom knows, so we'd better go in." I laughed, realizing that was the reason she'd been acting so weird with me earlier.

We drove down the driveway into the garage, and as we got out of the car, the door to the house flew open. Mom appeared holding a bottle of champagne and a camera. "Congratulations!" she cried, snapping a picture.

We call that picture "The Engagement Photo." Casey looks wide-eyed and slightly manic. I look stunned. Mom was beside herself with joy, unable to keep the secret a minute longer. It's a good thing Casey stopped in the driveway to pop the question, otherwise my mother would have beat him to the punch. She was so excited, she just couldn't help herself.

We went inside, opened the champagne, and stayed up late talking to Mom and Dad. Mom was eager to be in charge of the wedding planning, and I was glad to let her because I didn't have the time. The next day we flew to Columbus and told Casey's parents on Christmas Day.

It's a good thing my mom was such a great entertainer—not to mention being organized. I went back to work and turned over the affair to her. Our wedding took place on October 4, 1997, at 4:00 p.m. It was an unseasonably warm sixty-five degrees and brilliantly sunny. It was very special to be married by my grandfather in his church, where I'd grown up and where he'd married my mom. As he always had, my grandfather made it deeply personal, and I know my tears that day were in part because of the beautiful feeling of sharing this moment with him.

My heart swelled at being surrounded by my family and also by all the people who meant so much to me. Thelma sat at the piano, accompanying Benny Kim for a violin solo of "Adoration," by Felix Borowski, the first piece I'd ever performed in public. He also played "Méditation," by Jules Massenet, which had special meaning for me because my grandmother Hyllengren had often played it, as it was one of her favorites. Dorothy Benham, the 1977 Miss America from Minnesota, sang "Thanks Be to Thee" by Handel and "Because" by d'Hardelot.

My former teacher Jack Nabedrick read a passage from the Old Testament. My bridesmaids encircled me—the women who had meant so much during different times of my life. There was Molly, of course, and Kris, as well as my friend Chele from Stanford, and Karen from Cleveland. Then Patti, who orchestrated our first meeting, and Lisa, my colleague from Cincinnati. It was perfect in every way.

Our reception was held downtown at the Minneapolis Club, which was housed in a gorgeous old mansion. My mom had set up twinkling lights everywhere and the room looked magical. When we first arrived, we had a mini-crisis because my mom had overbooked. Even though the club only held 425 people, she had invited 440, telling me not to worry because we could expect a 10 to 20 percent drop-off, as if she were an airline booker. However, there was no drop-off—everybody showed up, and we had to jam a table in the hall. The kitchen was scrambling to come up with food for the extras—like salmon, which definitely wasn't on the menu.

Thelma's son Gordy was in a jazz band, and they played for the reception. It was a high-spirited, loving affair, but as the evening drew to a close I began to feel as if I was coming down with something. I had a double earache and a horrible sore throat. Luckily I got a prescription from Molly's dad before we left for our honeymoon.

Leave it to me, I was sick during my honeymoon. I had a terrible earache the day I visited the Vatican. But nothing could dampen the joy I felt being with Casey and knowing that with a wonderful job and a husband I loved, my life was as close to perfection as even a perfectionist like me could imagine.

Then I came home and got fired.

. . .

The Cleveland Indians were in the World Series that year, so we returned from our honeymoon to great fanfare in the city. They were up against the Florida Marlins, and the knuckle-biting series ended with the Indians losing in the seventh game. In spite of the disappointment of coming so close and then failing, the city of Cleveland threw the Indians a big parade after the series. Denise and I were scheduled to do a live broadcast sitting on top of a huge news truck, and it seemed as if the whole city was planning to attend.

A couple of days before the event I got a call from my agent, who told me the general manager wanted to see me after the parade. "Something might be up," she said.

"Do you know something I don't know?" I asked. She assured me she had no idea. I, of course, was suspicious. When the GM asks for a meeting, it's usually not good news.

What I remember most about parade day was feeling enormous pressure. It was probably the biggest event of my career in Cleveland, with the most potential viewers, and I had to perform flawlessly for hours on end while wondering if I was going to get fired. Performing under pressure was a familiar situation for me, and once again I called on that inner reserve I developed as a young girl on the stage. I made it through the day, showing a face of confidence and excitement to the viewers and the Indians fans. I'm sure no one guessed my inner turmoil.

Afterward, I returned to the station for my meeting. I walked into the general manager's office with every nerve on edge. My instincts were correct.

"The two-female anchor concept isn't working," he told me bluntly. "Unfortunately, we don't have another position for you at the station, based on your current salary level."

"Oh." My stomach clenched as I realized my worst fears were being realized. "What's going to happen to the broadcast?" I asked.

"Denise is staying on and we're replacing you with a man," he replied. Then he added, "Now that you're married, you'll be okay."

I was too stunned to respond, but later it was those words—*Now that you're married, you'll be okay*—that upset me. I was so disappointed that after I'd spent four years at his station, he still had no idea who I was. I was a professional who had dedicated years to establishing my career, and he had brushed me off with a gratuitous remark. I'd never heard of a man losing his job and being told, "Don't worry. You're married. You'll be okay." My career had zero to do with whether or not my husband also worked. It had everything to do with personal identity, personal goals, and making the most of my life.

In the early days after getting fired, I held myself together with the understanding that it was just an executive decision. One of us had to go and it was logical that I was the one. Denise was the hometown girl, she had been on air there for years, and everyone knew who she was. It never occurred to me that the media would portray it differently. I remember sitting in my house those first days and getting a shock as I read the headlines: "Bye-Bye Miss American Pie" and "There She Goes Miss America." I didn't understand why they were saying all those awful things about me. It hurt and felt humiliating.

I'd always thought of my career as a clear path, with all the moves and sacrifices serving a greater goal. I understood rationally that job security in the news business was nonexistent, but even when I'd made the risky move to the format of two female anchors, I hadn't given any real thought to what would happen if it didn't succeed. Now, derailed from my path, I felt stunned and alone. No one rushed to my support as I sat in the little house Casey and I had bought to start our new life. I discovered a sad truth that when you're fired people don't reach out to you, even though it's the time when you need them the most. I don't think it's because they're uncaring. They're just uncomfortable with sadness. They don't know what to say, so they say nothing. I've seen it happen for people who have lost loved ones, and it's the same distancing I experienced getting fired. People can't get past their own discomfort. The experience taught me an important lesson, and I now make a point of reaching out to people who are suffering a loss. I know how much it means to them.

My overwhelming emotion during that time was embarrassment. I had always been a perfectionist about everything I did, so now I thought of myself as a failure. It may not have been objectively true, but it was my emotional reality. I didn't want to leave the house, because I imagined people looking at me and thinking, "She blew it." The only safe place was my gym, where I rigorously worked out to keep my head on straight. Even in that relative haven, there were constant questions: "What are you going to do? Have you found anything yet?" I grimaced and said, "I'm working on it." And I was. I spent hours every day on my job search, calling every single person in my Rolodex, coming up empty.

That experience is the reason I've always had great empathy for people who are out of work. I understand the feelings of guilt and shame, which are mostly undeserved. I would never say that a jobless person didn't work hard enough or try hard enough to find work. I know better. I often think of all the people on the outside desperate to find a way back in, and my heart goes out to them.

The worst thing we can do is add to their sense of shame, which, trust me, is already great.

People often don't understand how the humiliation of getting fired can burrow into your consciousness for years to come, even when you go on to be successful. Long after I had reestablished my career and was doing well, I never told people I'd been fired. I have always believed that failure is necessary to success, but when it came to talking about this one big failure, I just couldn't do it. Then one day not so long ago, I was writing a motivational speech and the thought popped into my head: Why had I never talked about getting fired? I added the story to my speech, and I've openly talked about it on my show. The importance of reaching out to others and helping them get past their disappointments became more important than any residual shame I felt. But it took me a long time to get to that point.

Being newly married complicated things, because I knew I wouldn't be able to find a comparable news job in Cleveland. And I had my emotions to contend with. Casey and I were supposed to be in a honeymoon period, and suddenly we were in hell—or at least that's the way it felt to me. Casey tried to be supportive, but I was often frustrated with him, especially when he advised me to consider doing something different. "You're so talented, you can recreate yourself," he'd say. Or, "Why don't you go to law school? You always wanted to do that." Or, "Just start interviewing at companies. You could do something corporate." He meant well, but I resisted the idea that I should just give up on my chosen career because of one setback. God knows, I'd sacrificed plenty, moving three times already to follow my dream. I wasn't about to quit.

The question of identity was ever present. I was painfully aware that we most often define ourselves by our professions. People ask, "What do you do?" not "Who *are* you?" Yet if you define yourself by what you do or by how you look or any other external measure, you will collapse completely if you lose it. And that was what I experienced. Looking back, I wish I'd had the courage to pick up my violin during that year. I'd lost my way, but maybe I could have found it again if I had relied on the thing that was *me* through and through. Playing the violin was the closest I came to touching my soul, but at that point in my life it represented pain—the pain of my choices, the fear of my failure. So I left it in the case. At a time when I could have reclaimed the core of who I was—and let the beautiful notes lift me and move me—I chose to be fearful and unhappy. It was a missed opportunity. I wish I could go back and remake that year as a process of self-discovery with my violin. It was one of the biggest mistakes I've made.

My only goal was to get a job, and the opportunities were few. I had a chance with a station in San Francisco, but I knew that would be too big a move for my marriage, so I turned it down. Finally, after a year had passed and I was looking ahead to my second Christmas without work, I got an interview with a station in Dallas. Since I knew that my former boss and friend Kim Godwin-Webb was the news director at a competing station there, I called her. "I'm coming down to Dallas for an interview," I said. "You and I had a great relationship. Do you have anything for me?"

She said she might, so I headed to Dallas with two job interviews—an abundance of riches. When I got offers from both, I chose Kim's station, the NBC affiliate KXAS. I knew Kim respected me and we had a good relationship, and I liked the station. I was hired as a reporter and a weekend anchor.

Of course, accepting a job in Dallas meant that Casey and I would be separated after only one year of marriage. I'd never thought of myself as having a commuter marriage, but that's what we faced for nine months until Casey moved to Dallas. It wasn't easy, but we were both willing to do it. It sure beat me staying home crying! Moving to Dallas might not have been my first choice, but as I always tell kids today who want careers in the news, "If you don't want to pay the price, sacrifice, and have a lot of lonely nights, wondering, 'Why am I here and not making any money?' then don't go into this business."

I kissed Casey goodbye and moved to Dallas the week of Christmas, and I lived in a residence hotel for a month before getting an apartment. I was determined to make up for lost time and get back in the game. Gearing up for the new challenge, I pulled out my old pep talk, thinking, "Okay, here I go again. I'm going to work harder than anybody else, try and be the best that I can possibly be in this job, because here's my shot to be back in the game." It turned out to be an incredible experience, with opportunities to cover big regional stories for NBC. There were a lot of them during my time at KXAS. Columbine, the dragging murder of James Byrd, major tornadoes in Oklahoma. Under Kim's leadership I was also able to do important in-depth reports. The one I'm proudest of is the thirty-part series on domestic violence that led the evening news every night for a month, which earned me the American Women in Radio and Television "Best Series" Award. That series was a daring choice for a news division at the time and I learned so much as I was educating the viewers. Why do women stay in abusive relationships? Why don't they just leave? I came to understand the complexity of the issue and I was so proud to be the reporter allowed to dedicate so much time to it. I know in the end we saved many lives.

To my surprise, I came to love Dallas. It was a gleaming modern city, and the weather was great. It lived up to its reputation for be-ing big. Everything was supersized. My closet was bigger than most studio apartments in New York City! I was busy but lonely, missing Casey. The commuter end of the marriage didn't work out so well, because I worked weekends, which would have been the most log-ical time to travel. Add to that the fact that air travel between Dal-las and Cleveland was difficult, and we'd sometimes go several weeks without seeing one another. I was ecstatic when Casey moved to Dallas and we lived in the same place again. Together, we took advantage of all Dallas had to offer.

As the twentieth century came to a close, I covered the Y2K event. All the reporters were on duty New Year's Eve because people really believed that we might be facing a total technological collapse when the clock moved from 1999 to 2000. I was assigned to cover New Year's Eve from inside The Potter's House, the megachurch run by the evangelical superstar Bishop T. D. Jakes. There were thou-sands of people rocking the church that night, and after a few hours on the scene I started to get into the spirit of things. At one point, when the anchor tossed to me, I reached for an exclamation and came up with a chant borrowed from baseball games. "Let's get ready to rumble!" I cried as the clock ticked toward midnight. Inside the church the crowds roared, "Praise the Lord!" It was dizzying.

The world didn't end at midnight, and I finally crawled home at 4:00 a.m. Casey was up, ready to tease me. "Let's get ready to rumble?" he said, laughing. I defended myself, saying that was just the way the spirit moved me!

I took out my violin publicly once in Dallas, when I played "The Star-Spangled Banner" at a Texas Rangers game. They were playing the New York Yankees. Alone on the field with my violin, in front of a crowd of over forty thousand people, challenged by the wind and brutal acoustics, I gave my all to the anthem that resonates most deeply with Americans. In that performance I reached for my soul and left the field shaking with the beauty of the experience. Then I put my violin aside, but it continued to haunt me. In the years since, I've had a recurring dream: I am slated to perform at an important event. Taking the stage before a huge audience, I suddenly realize that I haven't practiced. I'm frozen with dread in the seconds before I wake up with a start. Lying in my bed with a pounding heart, I feel my violin calling to me. But I don't know if or when I'll pick it up again.

I always considered my years in the local markets—from Richmond to Cincinnati to Cleveland to Dallas—as preparation for the national stage.

When after less than two years in Dallas I got a job offer from CBS News in New York, I was elated. Getting a national network job was like going to the big leagues in baseball. Finally, all my hard work had paid off, and I was truly ready for the job. This time there was no family conflict about moving. Casey and I both wanted to pursue our careers in New York, which was the center not only of news but of sports.

Our first apartment was a ten-block walk from the office, and I loved the energy of the streets and being able to walk to work. In the beginning I thought I could wear my heels, but my shoes and feet were no match for the rough, cratered sidewalks of New York. I'd limp into the office with blisters and disintegrated heels. That's when I started following the example of other women on the street, wearing sneakers or flip-flops and carrying my heels in a bag.

I arrived in New York on the eve of the 2000 presidential election, and no sooner had I reported Hillary Clinton's New York

Senate victory on site at the Hyatt Hotel than I was packing my bags for Washington, D.C., where I'd be covering Al Gore during the recount crisis. Although the main action was in Florida, Gore was home in Washington and George W. Bush was in Texas while their lawyers and advisers fought it out. Along with many Americans, I came to wish I'd never heard the phrase "hanging chad." Still, like all reporters, I was thrilled to be at the center of the biggest political story of our times—a contested presidential election.

When I left for Washington, I told Casey, "I'll be back in a few days." Instead, I was in Washington, living at the Monarch Hotel, for weeks. Thanksgiving came and went, and the result remained up in the air. The Supreme Court ruling didn't come until December 12, more than a month after the election.

"Did *we* move to New York, or did *I* move to New York?" Casey asked me, only half teasing. What could I say? On the national stage, big news was always breaking—and I was there.

My job was for Newspath, a satellite service that delivered news for local affiliates to use in their broadcasts. It was an amazing training ground. I reported on the same stories that the CBS News correspondent was reporting for the national news, except my reports were seen on local stations—one after the other. The local broadcast would cue up the news item—for example, the execution of the Oklahoma bomber, Timothy McVeigh—and then the anchor would say, "Let's go live to CBS News correspondent Gretchen Carlson in Terre Haute, Indiana." I'd come on at the location and greet the anchor by name: "Hi, Cathy, in Indiana today, Timothy McVeigh . . ." Then I'd give my report, and finish, "Back to you, Cathy." On an average day I'd do thirty or more live shots, having to employ split-second timing.

My bags were always packed because I had to be ready to travel at a moment's notice. I covered the Vatican, the G8 Summit, the British royal family, the Super Bowl, and all the breaking news stories in between. I racked up more frequent flyer miles than when I was Miss America. It was exhilarating being on the scene for big news stories of the day. But the story that tested my mettle, as a reporter and as a person, was 9/11.

September 11, 2001, began as an ordinary day. Casey left the apartment early for his office a few blocks away. I was home getting ready to fly to Nashville to deliver a speech. I had just come out of the shower and was in the kitchen when the news broke of a plane flying into the World Trade Center. I called Casey to tell him about it, and he and a colleague went outside where they could look straight downtown. That's when the second plane hit.

I knew I wasn't going to Nashville. I called the office and they were summoning all the reporters in Manhattan to get there fast. I quickly got dressed and raced to CBS, where I learned that the Pentagon had been hit. My boss grabbed me and said, "I need you to go to the scene."

I was scared. "Do you know what will happen to us if we go down there?" I asked.

He shook his head, anxiety creasing his face. "No."

I went to my desk, and for the first time in my career I cried. I felt the unfathomable pain of the people lost that day, and to be honest I thought I was going to die that day too. I was sure I'd be swallowed up in the inferno of lower Manhattan. I called Casey and told him tearfully, "I don't know what's going to happen, but I have to go down there." Later, when people told me they admired all the brave reporters who rushed to Ground Zero to bring news of the attacks into American living rooms, I thought of my tears and how afraid I was. I wasn't an intrepid reporter at that moment. I was terrified. Still, I went.

As we sped downtown, the plumes of smoke rising in the air ahead of us, I could see waves of people streaming uptown. They were desperate to get away, and we were maneuvering to get closer. We couldn't get too close. Satellite trucks were set up on the West Side Highway, blocks from the site. Once on the scene, I forgot to be afraid and just started reporting. In the days that followed I filmed live reports from outside the pit, relaying the heartbreaking news that the courageous diggers on the pile were no longer looking for survivors, just bodies. I stood with my camera panning the hundreds of pleas tacked to walls and fences, trying to steady my voice and keep the tears at bay. Viewers didn't want to see a blubbering reporter on the screen. They craved information.

Working long days, trying not to be consumed by the horror around me, I'd arrive home late at night, covered with grime. The terrible smell clung to me even after a long shower. Only when I finally curled up in bed at midnight next to Casey did I turn on the TV and watch the reports. Then the full impact would hit me and I'd lose it, crying for all the heartsick mothers, fathers, children, friends, and lovers. Sleep would not come for a long time. I'd get up at 5:30 and go right back down there. More than any other story, 9/11 gave me a deeper appreciation for what it meant to be a journalist. When the nation is desperate and confused, you are their lifeline. I was exhausted, tense, and grief-stricken, but every single day I stood on the street, with a backdrop of pure horror, looked into the camera, and calmly reported what I saw and heard.

For those of us living and working in Manhattan, it could sometimes seem as if time had stopped and there would never be another story. But gradually normalcy resumed. When my time at Ground Zero ended, I had mixed feelings. I was emotionally connected to the downtown community, but I was also relieved to see that life had other dimensions besides horror and tragedy.

Soon after 9/11, CBS asked me to fill in on *The Saturday Early Show*. I was excited about the opportunity; it's something I had been angling for. Weeks before my debut I agonized about every detail, including what I would wear. I had many telephone conferences with my mother and finally settled on a powder blue Calvin Klein pantsuit.

I was so nervous that I didn't sleep at all the night before my first show, but it went well. After I filled in a few times, they offered me a permanent slot. I was thrilled to be coanchoring with Russ Mitchell, a real pro and a wonderful human being, who had been with CBS since 1992. He welcomed me warmly, showed me the ropes, and made me feel completely comfortable. I owe him a lot. A few years later Russ left CBS to become the lead anchor at WKYC in Cleveland, my old stomping ground.

I loved the morning show because it had a little bit of everything. Each broadcast opened with hard news. Then we'd move to interviews. There was a segment called the "Second Cup Café," which featured a musical performance. And we wrapped it up with cooking. My favorite segment was "Chef on a Shoestring," where we invited the great chefs of New York City to cook meals for under twenty dollars. It was a real perk to meet these chefs and dine at their restaurants. For one segment, Bobby Flay came to my apartment and I cooked for him. He was gracious and flattering, even when he found out I used crumbled Cheez-Its as the mystery ingredient for the top of my chicken divan.

The Saturday show was only one of my jobs. I also moved from Newspath to CBS News proper, and three days a week I reported for the *CBS Evening News with Dan Rather.* I was busy, but my life was more settled. I wasn't traveling as much. The stars were aligning for me to start a family.

CHAPTER 8

My Miracle Family

From the time I was a little girl, I always knew I wanted to be a mom and pictured myself having at least two or three children. Growing up in a loving family, I often thought about recreating the same kind of nurturing environment for my own kids. While I was building my career, I didn't worry about fertility. It was just a matter of timing, and I believed I had a wide window during my thirties to start my family. My women doctors reinforced this belief that fertility wasn't an issue for me. I never heard the truth, because everyone, including me, thought that women could have it all—a great career and a family—and there was no reason to cut my career advancement short. It was okay to wait to have children until I was established.

So when Casey and I decided the time was right, I had no concerns, even though I was thirty-five. Fertility ran in my family! My mom had four kids, and Kris, who was older than me, got pregnant right away. Piece of cake, right?

But after six months and no results, my doctor suggested I have a blood test to check the status of my eggs. The FSH (follicle-stimulating hormone) test is a noninvasive way of finding out how many eggs you have in reserve. A high FSH number signals a problem. It means that your system has to pump out more of the hormone because you don't have many eggs in reserve.

I couldn't believe it when my number came back high. The doctor casually remarked that I seemed to have prematurely aging eggs. "It doesn't mean you don't have one or two great eggs in there, but overall it doesn't look good." She recommended a fertility specialist.

Never in a million years had I expected this, and I was still in denial when I walked into the fertility doctor's Park Avenue office. When I sat down, he looked at my test results, frowning, and told me, "These numbers are not good at all. Have you considered a donor egg?"

"What? What do you mean?" I suddenly felt dizzy.

He patiently explained, "With numbers like these, the best option might be for you to consider a donor egg—that is, your husband's sperm and someone else's egg."

I fled, bruised by his cold indifference. He didn't even know me, and he was already farming out my pregnancy. I got out to the street, barely keeping it together. Sinking onto a bench across from the Plaza Hotel, I called my mother, sobbing. "Do you think that's what I'm going to end up doing?" She tried to comfort me, but honestly she didn't know the answer. "I don't want to have someone else's baby," I cried. "I want to have *my* baby."

But everywhere I went, doctors kept telling me it was a long shot. My chances of getting pregnant were deemed in the single digits. They decided to start me on a course of Clomid, a drug to encourage ovulation, but they said it probably wouldn't work. I kept thinking about my aging eggs and wanted to despair.

It was a very difficult time for me. I was heartbroken at the thought that I might never have children. Every day I came to work carrying a silent grief. Infertility is a private, secret problem. Only my doctors, those closest to me, and God knew about it. I later heard from many women who told me they didn't tell people about their struggles with fertility. There's a shame attached, an anguish that can't be shared. I prayed for acceptance, no matter what happened.

In the meantime, I was sent for an outpatient procedure called a hysterosalpingogram. It involves placing an iodine-based dye through the cervix and taking X-rays to help evaluate the shape of the uterus and whether the fallopian tubes are open or blocked. In the process it would "clean" my tubes—similar to blowing air into a clogged straw to get rid of dust.

The procedure was supposed to be no big deal—thirty minutes in and out. Casey was out of town on the West Coast, but my good friend Carrie Rabin, who was my field and segment producer at CBS Newspath, went with me. I refused the Valium they offered me in advance because I'd be returning to work. *Big* mistake. When they blew in the dye it felt as if a gun had gone off inside me. I screamed. It was the most pain I'd ever experienced, and I had barely recovered from the shock when a smiling doctor told me, "Good news, your tubes are clear."

It was full speed ahead for me to start taking Clomid at the beginning of my cycle, which was two weeks away. Casey and I were scheduled to take a cruise through Europe, and I had my supply of Clomid with me so I could start as soon as my period came.

We flew to Paris and I felt lousy the whole time. I had cramps and couldn't sleep. We did a tour of Normandy, which is amazing, but I felt sick the whole time. After boarding the ship in Normandy, we docked and wandered through picturesque villages in the Bordeaux region. In a cave in Saint-Émilion we came upon a chair carved of rock, which was said to be a fertility chair. Legend had it that a woman sitting in the chair and praying would become pregnant within two months. I hung back while the others on the tour went through. Then I sat in the chair and said a prayer.

Back on the ship I was still feeling unwell. My period was late, and suddenly it dawned on me that I should buy a pregnancy test. When we docked in Lisbon, I snuck off to a pharmacy. They didn't speak English, so I pantomimed, saying, "Le baby, le baby," and they finally figured it out. I took the test back to the ship. It is recommended that you take it first thing in the morning, and it was five in the afternoon, but I couldn't wait. Alone in the cabin I went into the bathroom and peed on the stick.

I sat on the bed and counted off the minutes, feeling scared about the result. I was so brainwashed about my lousy fertility at that point, I figured it would probably be negative. Finally, I got up my courage and crept back into the bathroom, hardly daring to look. And then I saw it—the blue line. I almost passed out. I was pregnant!

When Casey walked into the room I threw myself at him, waving the test and crying. "Look, look, the test is positive!"

The first words out of his mouth were, "We can't trust a Portuguese test!"

"Oh, come on," I said, not believing him. "It's a pregnancy test. You can't be half pregnant."

But Casey insisted we immediately go to the ship's doctor.

"What's the doctor supposed to do?" I asked grumpily. "I'll bet they don't even have pregnancy tests." I was right. The doctor cheerfully agreed to get a pregnancy test at a Lisbon pharmacy the next day.

As we walked out, I said, "Casey, you realize he's going to go to that same pharmacy that I was just at, don't you? The one you don't trust?" It was comical. Casey looked sheepish. I laughed. I didn't care. I *knew*.

The next morning I went to the doctor and took a second test. I was still pregnant! I couldn't even explain the miracle to myself. Maybe it was having my tubes "cleaned." Maybe I'd stopped worrying and relaxed because it seemed impossible. Who knows—maybe it was the fertility chair. Whatever the reason, I was thrilled. I e-mailed the fertility doctor who had recommended a donor egg, to tell him I didn't need his services after all. He wrote back that he was shocked.

I had met an amazing woman on the ship, a New Yorker named Dale Reiss. She was a top executive at Ernst & Young, and the first woman to be admitted to the New York Athletic Club. We liked each other immediately, and that night on the ship Casey and I had dinner with Dale and her husband. There was a storm and the ship was rocking and rolling, but I felt serene, not sick, because I knew I was pregnant. When the waiter came for our drink orders, I asked for sparkling water. Dale smiled at me and said, "Are you pregnant?" No alcohol—that was the giveaway. She was the first person to hear the news, even before my mother.

When we got home and called my parents, my mom just laughed. She thought I had a tendency to overdramatize things, and she said she'd always known that my fears about not getting pregnant were exaggerated. Easy for her to say.

Every pregnant woman goes through that uncomfortable early time when it just looks like you're gaining weight. When you're on national TV, it's a challenge to camouflage your pregnancy until you're ready to make the announcement. I wasn't at my most attractive, and my viewers might have noticed that I was wearing a lot of black. My motto: "Whatever fits that's black!" That included some unglamorous elastic waistbands. I gained fifteen pounds in the first trimester, so it was a lot of extra weight to hide.

In spite of my problems getting started, my pregnancy went smoothly. My sister had a baby six months before me, so she was my guide. In particular, she warned me that labor would take forever. I didn't want to hear that. I had my mother's impatience. Mom had often told the story about how she'd grown tired of sitting around waiting for me to arrive and had decided to go golfing. When she bent over to tie her shoes, her water broke. I arrived within hours, and she felt so good she ordered a meal.

When I went into labor on a Friday night, I recalled my sister's advice and figured I could still do my Saturday morning show before heading to the hospital. I told Casey, "It's going to take a long time. I'm going to go to bed for a while and I'll just get up and do the show."

"You're not doing the show!" he insisted.

"Yes, yes, the baby probably won't even come for another whole day."

By 2:00 a.m. I had changed my mind and asked Casey to call the show and tell them I wasn't coming.

I took a shower and we drove to the hospital around 6:00 a.m. I had a temperature, and the labor was progressing slowly. The doctor and nurses were coming in and out. I was worried, and asked if I was going to have a C-section. They kept saying no.

There was a TV on in the room, and my show was on from 7:00 to 9:00. Off the top they announced, "Good morning, everyone. Gretchen would love to be here. In fact, she thought she was coming to work today, but she's in labor having her baby right now." The nurses, realizing they were talking about me, said, "You were planning to go to work today?" Going to work didn't seem like such a great idea now.

I labored for the whole day, and then it suddenly became an emergency situation requiring a cesarean. "Five minutes!" the doctor shouted as they wheeled me into surgery. They'd already given me an epidural, so they upped the meds and rushed me into the operating room. I was awake the whole time and heard my baby's first cry.

Then they whisked her away and I didn't see her again for twenty-four hours. The doctors were concerned that I'd passed on a bacterial infection to her, and they took her to the neonatal intensive care unit. They wouldn't let me near her until my fever abated. Casey changed her first diaper and took Polaroid photos of her (this was before cell phone cameras) to bring down to me. I grumbled that I might as well have been in the hospital for knee replacement surgery. It didn't feel like I'd actually had a baby. Finally, when my fever dropped, they took me in a wheelchair to see Kaia.

She was beautiful—small and sweet with a fuzz of light hair. Her name is Scandinavian, meaning "wise woman." I loved this unusual, beautiful name. And I was completely in love with my tiny, darling girl, who happened to be the spitting image of my husband. We found Casey's newborn photo and took one of Kaia in the same position, and they were twins! However, I soon found out that she took after me in one important way: She had a big voice and didn't hesitate to make herself heard. It may have been a personality trait. But it's also called colic. I guess it was payback for driving my parents nuts with the same thing. In the early weeks I used to wheel Kaia around the apartment in her stroller to calm her down. If anyone had looked through the window they would have thought I was nuts. But I loved it. My maternity leave was only nine weeks and I was determined to make the most of every second.

They say that God never gives you more than you can handle, and my faith in that would be tested when Kaia was two months old. I was near the end of my maternity leave and was immersed in life with my daughter. One day I was sitting on the bed with Kaia perched next to me against a boppy pillow, looking sweet and content. As I gazed at her I caught a glimpse of an irregularity in her eye socket. At first I thought it was just the way the sun was hitting her face. But when I gently touched the area I detected a hard lump. I was immediately alarmed. I called Casey and then raced to the pediatrician.

She said the mass was probably one of three things. The best-case scenario was a cyst or a clogged tear duct. More serious would be an infantile hemangioma, a benign tumor of the blood cell lining. The worst-case scenario would be a cancerous tumor.

Thinking about the terrifying possibilities, I instantly went from being a joyful new mother to a dogged fighter on behalf of my helpless daughter. I was grateful that we lived in New York, where we could get in to see Dr. Francine Blei, a pediatric oncologist and hematologist at NYU Medical Center, who was considered the best in the field. She arranged an MRI, and Kaia was sedated. I stood by as my tiny daughter entered the cavernous machine. It was a painstaking process, because even sedated, Kaia would move. They had to start over several times.

When the test results came back, Kaia was diagnosed with an infantile hemangioma. These aren't rare, and they're usually not dangerous, depending on the location. Called "strawberry marks," they grow rapidly in the first year, before shrinking and even fading away completely over time. They commonly grow on the outside of the skin, on the back or head or on the hands. But Kaia's hemangioma was different. It was dangerous because it was located right near her eye. Growth forward threatened her vision, and growth backward her brain.

"Why did this happen?" I asked Dr. Blei. I wanted to know if I'd done something wrong or, worse, if there was a genetic component that might also affect future children.

She answered that no one knew why these spontaneous growths occurred. They could have a genetic component if there are vascular anomalies in your family. Mostly it seemed to be the luck of the draw. Hemangiomas can't be detected in utero, but after birth they grow as the infant grows. Statistically they happen more often in girls by a four-to-one margin and are more prevalent in Caucasians.

It was frustrating to be without answers about the cause, but I was ready to be fully engaged in the treatment. Unfortunately, not much could be done. Surgery was out of the question because it was a blood tumor and an operation would cause fatal bleeding. So we had few options. In the beginning the decision was to just watch it carefully to evaluate the growth pattern. Nearly every day I left work to take Kaia for eye exams. Since we were at the top clinic in the nation, the waiting room was always crowded with families who had come from all over the world to seek treatment. Many of the children were terribly disfigured by the tumors and were much worse off than Kaia, which put things in perspective.

Still, strangers weren't always so kind about the way our daughter looked. Patricia, our wonderful Jamaican babysitter, was beside herself most days. "I don't know what to tell people," she cried with anguish. "They say, 'Why does your baby look funny? What's wrong with her?'" I told her to ignore it. She was under no obligation to tell strangers anything.

I fought panic every day, but sometimes it overwhelmed me. I remember a desperate call to my mother where I cried, "I didn't think I could have a baby, and now my baby might go blind!" She immediately got on a plane to New York. As always, she was there with support when I needed it.

As the months passed, the tumor grew, forming a pretty big knot. When it started pushing Kaia's eyelid down, beginning to impair her vision, we reached a crossroads. Doctors recommended a course of steroids, and Casey and I went home to make the biggest decision of our lives.

Giving steroids to an infant comes with scary risks. We learned that steroid treatment could have lifelong ramifications, such as impaired cognitive function, stunted growth, and poor motor skills. Not to mention the short-term effects, which included extreme irritability and a swollen moon face. On the other end of the scale, without steroid treatment our daughter could become blind. We had no real choice. We agreed to the steroids in order to save Kaia's eyesight, but we were filled with dread.

Each morning as I approached Kaia's crib with the liquid medicine, she looked up at me trustingly, laughing and kicking her feet.

She liked the grape flavor. But it broke my heart to fill the vial and give it to her—every single time.

On steroids, Kaia was a holy terror, manic and out of control. She was so bad that she once got kicked out of the Barnes & Noble reading room. Patricia was beside herself when she told me the news, but I laughed so hard I cried. With an odd pride I called Casey and said, "Your eight-month-old daughter got thrown out of Barnes & Noble today." Then I told Patricia not to worry about it. This too would pass.

Casey and I showered Kaia with love, our little moon-faced terror. When we looked at her, we didn't see the swelling or the tumor or the pirate eye patch. We saw only our beautiful child.

And the steroids seemed to be working. The tumor was shrinking. We began to wean Kaia off the medicine. We were ready to put that chapter behind us, and we couldn't detect any of the worst side effects in Kaia. She seemed to be normal.

But shortly after we discontinued the steroids, the hemangioma came roaring back bigger than it had been before. We began the process again, with a revived fear of the potential damage the medicine might cause. Fortunately, the second course of steroids worked, and we watched Kaia's tumor fade to a thin blue vein. In the years that followed, we stayed alert for any signs of cognitive delay or impaired motor skills, and they never came. Kaia grew into a lovely, smart, talented young lady with no ill effects from the trauma of her first year. We were blessed.

In the midst of the special challenges of Kaia's infancy, I also entered the strange world of the working mom. CBS was wonderful about giving me time to take Kaia to doctor's appointments, but I still had a job to do, and being a new mom presented challenges of its own. Any woman who has ever had to pump breast milk at work knows exactly what I'm talking about. It's a nightmare that consumes your life. I was lucky to have a private office at CBS, but people still knew what I was doing in there, because the machine was so loud. Debbye Turner, whom I'd crowned Miss America, was two doors down, and when I'd start pumping, she'd e-mail me, "The drone is on." She could hear the whirring noise coming from my office. We always had a good laugh about that.

There was also the issue of where to store the milk once it was pumped. I didn't want to put it in the common refrigerator where people kept their lunches. So I bought a mini-refrigerator, and also a mini-microwave so I could heat up my lunch to eat in the office while I pumped. Almost immediately a fuse blew and the lights went out on our entire floor. I knew I was the culprit, but I didn't rush to own up.

The director of operations came into my office. "Do you have any devices in here?" he asked, looking around.

"Devices?" I asked innocently.

He spotted the microwave and the refrigerator and admonished me for nearly taking down the power grid at CBS. He let me keep the refrigerator, though.

I had to wash the pump suction parts in the common bathroom when I was done, so three times a day I put them in a Starbucks bag and carried them to the bathroom. It was time-consuming, messy, and frustrating. My heart goes out to all the new moms out there who are pumping away in offices across America.

A lot of working mothers talk about feeling guilty every minute they're away from their children. The truth is, it doesn't matter if you're working outside the home or not, in our society guilt seems to be an acceptable mode for mothers—period. Well, I don't buy it. Instead of wasting time on guilt, it's more important to be clear in your own mind and heart about what kind of person you want to be, and that includes what kind of parent you want to be. It's a very personal choice. I always knew that I would be a mom with a career, and I aspired to pass on to my children a living example of what it means to follow your dreams and be a fulfilled human being. I've always said that being a mom was my most important role, but it's not my *only* role. I've been gratified and humbled when other mothers with careers have told me I'm a model for them.

That's not to say that the stress levels and sleep deprivation weren't off the charts sometimes. (As comedian Amy Poehler, mother of two, put it, "Tired is the new black.") I'm not ashamed to admit that there were some days early on when I couldn't wait to get to work.

One reason I felt so confident was that I had a partner in parenting who was completely there for us. Casey was a rock during Kaia's difficult first year. He was the solo parent on the weekends because I worked Saturday and Sunday. He loved it, even when he threw his back out bouncing Kaia on a medicine ball to try to get her to settle. It helped that we were on the same wavelength. I credit our shared midwestern sensibilities and strong values for getting us through the tough times.

We also talked about our roles and responsibilities. Hard as it is to believe, many couples don't do this. I have heard the experts advise—and I support this completely—that couples should have the big conversation about shared responsibilities before they get married, and especially before they have kids. We talked and talked. Casey wanted to be fully involved—and he has been. My tendency is to see the scary side of things first, and Casey is much more laid-back and easygoing. When Kaia was going nuts on steroids, he was amazingly calm. Thanks to Casey, we got through it, and I actually flourished in those years at CBS because of his support. I was able to grow in my profession because I knew that he had my back.

Having said that, let's be real. The truth of the matter for all moms, whether they work outside the home or not, is that most of the parenting responsibilities are on our shoulders. This is partly our fault because we try to be in control and tend to be super critical when our husbands don't do things exactly our way. We think we can do it better, so we correct our husbands or say, "Oh, forget it. I'll do it myself." I put myself in that category, and it's something I've had to work on. It doesn't matter if the baby is dressed in stripes and polka dots as long as she's healthy and safe! If we're going to ask for fifty-fifty cooperation, we have to give up the need to be the boss. Humor doesn't hurt. When a worried mom asked me at a panel discussion how she could convince her husband to take on more of the chores, I replied—to roars of laughter—"I would recommend a glass of wine and a hot tub."

These days there's an ongoing debate about whether women can "have it all," and I've often been asked that question. In fact, the first time was at the Miss America pageant. I was the only one who said no. I didn't mean that women shouldn't fully pursue their dreams, only that we need to be honest with ourselves. I'm a person who likes to give 100 percent to everything I do. I want to be the best at my job and as a mother. But I realize I can only give 100 percent in the moment. If I'm at work, am I giving 100 percent to my kids? No. If I'm at home, am I giving 100 percent to my work? No. It's a balancing act, but worthwhile as long as we don't kid ourselves that we're superwomen.

Undeterred by my fertility challenges, I was plotting my next pregnancy. I was determined to have at least one more child—against all odds. If my eggs were old when I conceived Kaia, they were now *really* old. I couldn't fool around. It was now or never.

I found a new fertility doctor, because I wasn't about to go back to the "donor egg" guy. He did tests and found that my egg count had gotten a little worse, but it was not impossible. When he suggested the tube cleaning test, I looked at him as if he had three heads. No way was I going through that awful procedure again! But he assured me he was really good at it. "I promise it won't hurt."

"That's like telling me a gunshot won't hurt. Explain again why it's so important."

He told me that in his experience, a high proportion of women got pregnant within two months of having the test. "It cleans out their tubes, even though they're open, and it just works."

That was convincing, but I was still scared.

"Trust me," he said, and I did.

This time Casey was with me, and I took two Valium. I was awake during the procedure and I watched on a screen as the dye went in. I didn't feel a thing. And I got pregnant that month.

At first I didn't know I was pregnant. It was June, and on my birthday I was feeling depressed because I'd spotted that morning. I had the day off, and I went to a nearby diner, ordered tea, and sat there feeling miserable and teary-eyed.

As I sipped my tea, a thought entered my mind that wouldn't go away. I felt so lousy—maybe I was pregnant. I got up and went to the pharmacy and got a pregnancy test. Casey was taking me out for my birthday that night, and before we left, I went into the bathroom and did the test.

Positive!

Filled with excitement, I got dressed for dinner, deciding I'd give Casey the news at the restaurant. When the waiter took our drink orders, I said, "Just sparkling water."

Casey looked at me with a raised eyebrow. "Are you pregnant?" he asked. There it was again—the alcohol giveaway.

The story of my pregnancy with Christian is about false positives on tests. The first was my amniocentesis at sixteen weeks. I was told it looked like the fetus had a hole in his spine.

I knew something about this. I'd been volunteering for the March of Dimes since I was sixteen. A hole in the spine meant spina bifida. The doctor assured me it wasn't conclusive until they performed a second test. I had to wait three weeks, and instead of freaking out, I was strangely calm and focused. I'd just been through a terrible year with Kaia, and I thought, "If I made it through that, I'll make it through this." I spent long hours on the phone and the computer, researching spina bifida. I wanted to be prepared for what my family would face.

Three weeks later, the verdict came in: false alarm. No hole in the spine. Elation doesn't even begin to describe it! But then it happened again.

At my twenty-week ultrasound, the doctor, looking grave, showed Casey and me a picture. "A normal brain would look like this . . ." Uh-oh, I thought, taking Casey's hand and squeezing. I thought I was going to lose it. The doctor explained that our baby had "spots" on the brain, and this was often seen with trisomy 7, which the amniocentesis tests for. We'd cleared the trisomy 7 through amniocentesis, and even though the doctor assured us the spots on the brain would go away, we had to live with the uncertainty until he was born. They really mess with your mind with those tests. I told my mother, "If I ever get pregnant again, I'm not going to have any tests, because they serve no purpose except to scare the hell out of me."

Other than the tests, it was a normal pregnancy in all respects. But even when Christian was born, the doctors hovered around saying he didn't look right and his "tone" was off. He had a brain scan when he was a day old and was seen by neurologists, who worried he might have epilepsy. At the very least, they warned me that he might be a challenge.

A final false alarm. As it turned out, Christian has been an amazing kid, not difficult at all, but very high-energy. He's also smart as a whip, and he makes me laugh every day. He has a boundless optimism. My favorite image of Christian is flat on his butt at the ice rink for his first skating lesson, yelling to me at the top of his lungs from the center of the rink, "Mommy, look at how fantastic I am at skating!"

I am constantly in awe of what unique individuals my children are. While Christian is the kidder, Kaia has always been a lot more serious, even when she was little. One night when she was four, I told her that I had to go into work extra early in the middle of the night because there was breaking news. "What time?" she asked. I said, "Three-ten." That morning, as I tiptoed down the stairs, I heard Kaia's small voice. "Mommy, you're late. It's three-thirteen." Do you think she takes after her mom a little bit?

Having children is the most amazing experience of life. I find myself just looking at them when they are reading or sleeping and thinking how incredibly lucky I am and blessed to have them. The cherub faces never get old.

The most wonderful thing about children is their great curiosity and complete honesty. I would love to capture those priceless moments in the years before they grow up and become guarded and stop sharing every little thing that's on their minds, even when the questions elicit chuckles or embarrassment on the part of the adults.

Like Kaia at three when we would end our nightly prayers with "Amen," looking confused and asking, "Mommy, why at the end of our prayers do you always say, 'Old Men'?" Or at five on my parents' anniversary asking Grandma Karen, "Are you going to have any more babies?"

Or Christian at eight, observing that he thought a woman at the pool had fake boobs. When I picked myself up off the floor and asked him what he meant, he explained, "Well, I knew that they weren't real because, um, like yours, when you bend over, they like fall all the way down. And hers, when she bent over at the pool, Mom, they didn't move." Christian is always bursting with curiosity, asking questions we don't necessarily want to answer—like the time he saw an ad during a baseball game and asked, "Mommy, what's Viagra?"

By the time my maternity leave with Christian ended, I was experienced at being a working mom, but this time it was different. I wasn't just returning to work. I had a whole new gig: I was moving to Fox News.

Although I loved working for CBS, it was pretty clear that the higher-ups weren't interested in giving me a five-day-a-week opportunity on the morning show in the foreseeable future, and my dream was to host a national daily morning show. That was a distinct possibility at Fox, and just as important was the prospect of working for Roger Ailes. I thought Ailes was brilliant. He was the first person in the television world to put opinion shows in prime time, and it was working. He figured out that viewers were getting their news during the day from a variety of different formats—TV, newspapers, radio, and increasingly the Internet. So by the time people were home from work and settling in for the night, they already knew a lot of the news of the day. Now they wanted to be entertained and to hear analysis and opinion, even if they didn't always agree with what was said. Ailes successfully developed a powerful nighttime lineup for viewers that set cable on its head—and is still dominating the airwaves today.

In person Roger was razor sharp and inscrutable, and we seemed to have a real connection. He saw something in me that he liked—what he called my "killer instinct." He once noted that I would stop at nothing to do the job. He *got* me. Over the years I've come to value our time together. He encourages me to be myself, to relax, and to not try so hard to look smart. "People know you're smart," he says. He was also the first person to urge me to talk about being Miss America. CBS had taken the reference off my résumé, and I had come to see it—unfortunately—as not especially good for my credibility. Roger insisted people wanted to hear about Miss America from time to time, and that was certainly a pleasant shock. The subject didn't come up that often, but I no longer felt that it was a part of my biography that had to be ignored or hidden. From the start I realized that working at Fox News was going to be different than anything I'd ever done.

CHAPTER 9

Woman
in the Middle

I like to joke that when I joined Fox News I hit the "bimbo trifecta": *Former Miss America. Blonde. Fox News host.* I say that with tongue in cheek, but I may have achieved a Google record for being called dumb or a bimbo. I can joke about it, because it doesn't take a rocket scientist to understand that the characterization has more to do with silly attitudes and stereotypes than with who I am or whether or not I'm smart. I still scratch my head trying to figure out how being blonde became synonymous in some people's minds with being dumb, or why attractive women are assumed not to be smart, but I don't waste my abundant brain cells trying to figure these things out. I've learned that sometimes when people don't like what you have to say, and don't want to debate you on ideas, it's just easier to call you a dumb blonde from Fox News.

Long before I started working for Fox, I had to put up with the dumb blonde label, based solely on having been Miss America. Never mind that I'd graduated with honors at Stanford or studied at Oxford. The stereotype is as old as the pageant. Mostly I ignored it.

I tried to avoid the trap of doing things to "prove" I was smart, but when I was asked to be a contestant on *Jeopardy!* for the "Power Players" week shortly before I moved to Fox, I was happy to do it. It was a week of shows with news media and Washington, D.C., folks, with the money going to charity. Maybe a tiny part of me was thinking it would be a good opportunity to show that I could compete on the level of pure knowledge, but mostly I thought it would be fun. As you know by now, I love to compete.

I called the producers and asked what I could do to prepare. Their only advice was, "Watch the show." But since I've always been big on preparation, I bought the home version, with thirty-four games and an answer book. During my lunch breaks at work, and on vacation in Arizona, I quizzed myself on the arcane details of sports, literature, science, American history, state capitals, land masses, authors, presidents, Shakespeare—the list goes on. I lay awake at night mentally scrolling through planets and state capitals. A friend kindly suggested that maybe I was going too far when I started listing state trees over dinner one night. (Minnesota? Red pine!)

Then I showed up at the studio and saw that I was up against two formidable—and experienced—contenders: MSNBC's Keith Olbermann and Al Franken, who at that time was a comedian, author, and radio show host. (A few years later Franken would successfully run for the Senate in Minnesota.) Both had competed on *Jeopardy!* before—Franken twice. I was the newbie. But I made it through the practice round, and even won the practice Final Jeopardy.

The first thing I have to say about *Jeopardy!* is that it's as much about finger work as it is about brainwork. Thank God for all that video game practice! The buzzer is the key to everything. It's a nickel-sized white contraption, and your finger fits on top of it, allowing you to buzz in at the right second. It's tricky. If you buzz in before Alex Trebek is finished reading the question, you get frozen out. Otherwise, you have a millisecond to beat your competitors to the buzzer. It's all about the rhythm.

Al Franken won the game, and $50,000 went to the Congressional Hunger Center. I wasn't embarrassed; it was all in good fun.

At one point someone suggested that I was deliberately "dumbing down" my material on *Fox & Friends*. Okay, so now I wasn't really dumb, I was just pretending! Even Jon Stewart got into the act, chiding me by way of listing my impressive credentials. I actually got a kick out of that, because the subliminal message was that I was smart. But to this day, if I make the tiniest error, Twitter lights up with the dumb blonde narrative. I'm used to it.

It's ironic that these so-called bimbo sightings happened so often during my seven years on *Fox & Friends*, because it takes considerable skill and smarts to be on live TV for three hours every day. It's not just two males and a female hanging out on the "curvy couch." For one thing, being on cable TV is a whole different experience than working for network TV. It's far less scripted. You have to have a depth of knowledge to talk back and forth for three hours. The show's definitely all about chemistry, and it's not something you just walk into and know how to do the first day. You don't. You can be the smartest person in the world and you could still be challenged by the format of the show.

But the "dumb" label was hard to shake. By the way, that's true of all of my female colleagues at Fox News. I felt we were somewhat vindicated in 2013 by a blog post on the Web site PeppermintFarm titled "The Dumb Girls of Fox," which hit the nail on the head. The introduction read in part, "The next time you hear someone criticizing Fox News for supposedly having a 'bunch of dumb gals' as eye candy . . . check out their qualifications . . . let them speak for themselves!" What followed was a rundown of the women of Fox News and their remarkable credentials, including multiple degrees and impressive achievements. The post ended with a challenge: "So liberals, progs, Alinskyites, when you want to throw rocks take a look at yourself in the mirror. Try to find that many highly intelligent women on your alphabet station. How many degrees do your women reporters have?"

The fact of the matter is, live TV means always being on your toes. Shortly after I joined Fox News, I was filling in on an afternoon show when there was breaking international news. Now, you have to understand that on Fox we cover much more international news than you'd typically see on the networks, and some of it was relatively obscure to the average person. So when I heard in my earpiece, "A fugitive wanted for questioning in the assassination of former Lebanese prime minister Rafic Hariri was arrested in Brazil," I can't say I was knowledgeable about the story. When the producer then said in my ear, "Just go with this for three minutes," it felt like being back on *Bloopers and Practical Jokes*. It goes to prove that it's always good to stretch yourself, and that life is all about learning, experiencing new challenges, and always improving.

One day I had a dramatic experience along with my old friend and colleague from Cincinnati, Bill Hemmer. I was filling in at the anchor desk when we started covering one of those heartstopping car chases. When Bill came on the air, we tag-teamed it, ping-ponging comments across the studio. The video was on the car chase, with our voice-overs doing a blow-by-blow. We had to keep up a constant banter, and believe me, it wasn't easy. It's called "going wall to wall." Suddenly, everything else is blown out. Behind the scenes they were scurrying to find guests we could talk to so we wouldn't just be sitting there. I remember having a second to look up and over at Bill, who was sitting at another desk, raising my eyebrows like, "What are you going to say?" I didn't have a moment to breathe, but later I thought how surreal it was that Bill and I were back together at Fox. A long way from Cincinnati.

I had been at Fox News for a year when I was tapped to replace E.D. Hill on *Fox & Friends*, Fox's signature morning show. All I could think was that I had big shoes to fill. E.D. had been with the show since its inception in 1999, and she was loved by the viewers. Like me, she had a strong journalism background, and she did many important stories and was a great interviewer. It was a fast switch. E.D. left the show on a Friday and I was there on Monday. I had finally achieved my lifelong goal of doing a national morning show five days a week.

When I first started on *Fox & Friends* I only did the 7:00 to 9:00 hours, and it was somewhat manageable, but when I signed a new contract they told me, "We have good news and bad news. The good news is you're doing a great job and we'd like you to now start at 6:00 a.m. and do three hours. The bad news is we'd like you to now start at 6:00 a.m. and do three hours." At first this was a bit of a struggle for me. A lot of TV people would have jumped at the chance to have more "face time." But I had two small children at home and was barely getting enough sleep as it was. We'd moved to Connecticut, so my commute went from rolling out of bed and being at the office in five minutes to a fifty-minute drive—when there wasn't traffic. Getting up an hour earlier seemed like too much, so I developed a plan that allowed me to get up only a half hour earlier. I moved all of my clothes home so I could get dressed there instead of at the office, thus saving time. And I had my prep papers waiting for me in the hair room, so I didn't have to go down to the newsroom first.

Strategy was everything when it came to my schedule. I had it down to split-second timing, setting three alarms to be up at exactly 3:50 a.m. (I never once overslept.) I showered, brushed my teeth, pulled my wet hair into a ponytail, threw on the clothes that I'd laid out the night before, grabbed my bag sitting at the front door, and was out of the house in nine minutes flat, where a car was waiting. I studied like crazy on the drive into the city, arriving at 5:00 for hair. While my hair was being done, I kept studying, going through massive piles of newspapers and articles, throwing what I didn't need into the trash can beside me, scribbling notes in the margins like I did in class at Stanford. Into makeup at 5:30, where no studying could happen. She needed my eyes. Listened to music and got into a good frame of mind for the show. At 5:55, after the last eyelash and lip gloss—lots of it—was applied, raced out to the freezing cold set, and at 6:00 on the dot said, "Good morning, everyone. I'm Gretchen Carlson. Thanks for sharing your time with us today."

I was always confident, knowing I had a strong team behind me. I can't emphasize enough how doing great TV is all about that team—the floor crew, the producers, the bookers, the directors, the assistants, the hair and makeup people. They made the show every single day. I've always had a good relationship with everyone behind the scenes, because I respect how much they do. Viewers only see the people on camera. They have no idea what goes on beyond camera range. I always love bringing guests to the set so they can see a terrific team at work.

The essence of live TV is that once it's done it's in your rearview mirror. We walked off the set and were already thinking about tomorrow.

After the show there were meetings, interviews, and prep for the next day before I could finally start my long commute home. If I was lucky, I'd get out of the office by 1:00 p.m. But I always had lots of extra stuff to do. For example, there were stacks of requests for autographed photos, and I made a point of personally responding to every one of them, including addressing the envelopes myself. It's a practice I continue to this day. It takes discipline not to get behind. When I told a friend about this, she said, "Oh, I always assumed you used one of those autographing machines or had an intern do it." Not so. Every autograph is from my own hand.

I also believe it is very important to write letters and notes. Really, even in this age of texts. It's a habit that goes way back for me. When I was Miss America, doing an appearance at a mall in Ohio, they wheeled in a man who was quite disabled and confined to a cot. It meant so much for Jim Demuth to meet me. He had trouble speaking, but when he asked if I would be his pen pal, I was so moved that I said yes. I corresponded with him every month for twelve years until he died in 2001. It was meaningful for both of us.

If you want to make a difference in people's lives, write to them. A few years ago, when my executive producer's brother died unexpectedly, I wrote her mother a letter, even though I didn't know her. When my executive producer went home last Christmas to help her mother after she had a stroke, she noticed that my letter was still sitting there next to a photo of her son. It mattered to her. I hope to instill in my children that it matters to people when you make the effort to reach out to them. And it's also a piece of advice I share with young people in the business. Always send a note, write a letter—let people know you mean it by taking the time to make that special effort. I was pleased to find out that Roger Ailes is also a big believer in handwritten notes. To honor that, I still write him notes frequently instead of e-mails.

Ever since I was a child musician and had to be efficient about using every hour of the day, I'd never napped, and I didn't now. So I had to plan an early bedtime in order to get enough sleep to power through the day with a full-time job at Fox and a full-time job as Mom.

It took me a while to find my voice. *Fox & Friends* was different than anything I'd ever done—a carefully calibrated mix of entertainment and news. It was certainly not like the other morning shows. But I soon got into the rhythm. Doing the show every day, I not only built my knowledge base, but I got comfortable. I learned you can get used to anything—even getting up at 3:50 in the morning. I always had a lot of sympathy for guest hosts who filled in for me when I was away, because it's hard to jump in and pick up the rhythm of a show that requires a deep knowledge base about news stories, chemistry among the hosts, and ad-libbing.

Sitting in the middle, flanked by Steve Doocy on the right and Brian Kilmeade on the left, I had to speak not only as the lone woman, but also as the journalistic voice, with fifteen years of hard news experience. I teasingly called Steve and Brian my "work husbands" because I spent more time with them than I did with Casey.

We each had our roles to play on the show. For example, Steve might be the one to outline the facts of a story we were about to discuss. Brian had a passion for military issues, and we had many discussions about the wars in Iraq and Afghanistan. My role was often to say, "Now that we know all that, what does it mean?" I think it might surprise people that we didn't work out what we would say in advance. I never saw Steve or Brian until I came flying out onto the set with three seconds to spare. After a time, we all had a pretty good idea of where each other stood, but I did enjoy throwing a curve, usually on cultural issues.

We were distinct personalities, too. Steve has an uncanny ability to connect with the audience. He can be very serious, but he has a fun side, which he'd showcase on forays out to the plaza. He could talk to ordinary people and draw them in. Brian is one of the hardest-working people I've ever met. He never sleeps! In addition to *Fox & Friends* he has a three-hour radio show every day. Then he goes home and virtually inhales the news, watching every program. Of course, as the viewers well know, Brian also has a funny side. He's quick-witted and not afraid to throw himself into the fray. Throughout my time on *Fox & Friends*, Brian kept me in stitches.

I used to tell people that the reason I sat in the middle on *Fox & Friends* was because I'm a registered independent. That label says it all: I think for myself. Sometimes people were surprised, as if the idea of being at Fox News and being an independent was an impossible stretch.

Once, when I was a guest host on *The View*, we somehow got on the topic of political differences and air kissing. Joy Behar said that she had kissed a lot of Republicans, and I asked, "Do you kiss independents, since I'm an independent?" Joy seemed stunned. At the commercial break she turned to me and said, "You're not a Republican? I thought you had to be a Republican to work at Fox." One more misperception bites the dust.

The other misperception was that I may not have a sense of humor about people making fun of the show, but honestly, I just loved the spoof that *Saturday Night Live* did of *Fox & Friends*. I laughed my head off when I saw the portrayal Vanessa Bayer did of me. One day my makeup artist, who also does makeup for *SNL,* told me that Vanessa was always asking, "Is Gretchen mad at me?" I said, "No, I'm not mad at her. Tell her I'm a fan." And I was. I've always enjoyed laughing at myself, and I even felt a little bit flattered that I had "made it" enough to be spoofed on *SNL*.

News and politics were a big part of *Fox & Friends,* but there were also a lot of lifestyle and entertainment segments. We went from serious to funny to working out on the air. I was able to say to my mother, "Look, Mom, now people can see all sides of my personality!"

I was the one to jump rope and do push-ups with members of the military—except I was in a dress, although I took off my shoes. Jumping rope was my specialty, because when we first moved to New York, Casey and I went to a jump-roping gym and got into it. At that point I only knew how to do slow jumping, but I learned to do fast jumping, kind of like Rocky in training. I was so determined to learn that I practiced in our apartment, and Casey thought I was nuts, but I mastered it to the point where I could do thirty minutes straight. It was crazy good exercise.

We had animal segments—Jack Hanna, the wildlife guy, made regular appearances—and I always volunteered to do those. One day we had a kinkajou on set. It's a rain forest creature a little like a miniature kangaroo. It jumped into my hair and started licking my ear, swishing its furry tail into my eyes. Ugh! Another time Jack Hanna brought a dangerous cobra onto the set. It was in a basket with a lid on it, and there was a hook to handle the snake. Brian just decided to grab the hook and remove the lid. The snake started pouring out of the basket, and Jack Hanna jumped onto the sofa because this particular snake could kill you. Seeing its head and body weaving out of the basket was like watching a horror movie. I ran off the set and you could hear me screaming in the background, "Brian! Brian, put the snake back into the basket!" Meanwhile, Jack Hanna was up on the couch trying to call 911.

Roger Ailes, the most accessible boss I've ever worked for, was behind the scenes. He saw Fox as a big family, and he cared about everything we did. Sometimes he'd show up in the control room or call during the show. He'd watch us at six before he left home and then listen in the car going to work. One day we had set up a batting cage outside the building and were doing a segment where we all tried to hit eighty-mile-an-hour pitches. Roger walked by on his way into the office and he stopped at the batting cage and took a crack at the ball. On live TV! Roger always has the capacity to surprise.

The most challenging part of the show was the political interviews, but I loved doing them. I became known for my fiery interviews. Like the one I did with then Press Secretary Robert Gibbs. He did his best not to answer my questions. Par for the course, but it turned contentious. The interview was in advance of a big speech President Obama was giving that night talking about the end of the Iraq war. I asked Gibbs whether the president was planning to explain his flip-flop on the surge to the American public. Gibbs instantly went into attack mode: "I think what's important, while you guys play political games, is [for] the president to laud our men and women, and to mark the end of our combat mission." Believe me, I wasn't the one playing political games. When I asked him whether Obama would credit Bush in his speech, Gibbs basically refused to answer—so I just kept asking. Frustrated, he said, "Gretchen, I don't know whether this is you actually interviewing me or just a tape of you looping the same question over and over." Well, that's what I do when I don't get answers.

I interviewed all the presidential candidates in 2008 and 2012, along with other political luminaries, and I enjoyed those interviews. One morning I interviewed eight candidates all in one show. Sometimes political figures could be like rock stars and it took extra effort. I'd arranged an interview with Sarah Palin while she was doing her bus tour in Florida. It took six months to set up a seven-minute interview. It was the day before Thanksgiving, and it so happened that I was going to Disney World with my whole family, and I ended up not going to the park with my kids one day so I could do the interview. It was at the huge retirement community, The Villages, and I was on the stage with Palin, and the interview was piped out to thousands of people in the Barnes & Noble parking lot outside. The interview was simultaneously being fed back to New York.

The next morning I was doing the show live from Orlando, and that night Kaia lost her first tooth. I told Casey, "I have to go to bed, so you need to make sure to put a dollar under Kaia's pillow so it will be there when she wakes up in the morning."

When I got up at the crack of dawn, I just happened to peek under Kaia's pillow and the tooth was still there. No money. Casey forgot. I ran and grabbed a dollar bill, retrieved the tooth, and shoved the money under her pillow before I went to take a shower. Literally three seconds later, Kaia woke up and reached under her pillow. Talk about split-second timing!

Of course, Kaia being Kaia, she was quite concerned about losing her tooth. She asked me, "Mommy, are people going to say, 'Who's the funny little girl without any teeth?'" Stifling a laugh, I patiently explained to her that all children lose their baby teeth before they get their adult teeth, and nobody would think she looked funny—just like a regular girl.

For me, the biggest thrill of being on live TV is the adrenaline rush that comes from doing breaking news. It's what every broadcaster lives for. I found that it was in the midst of a breaking news story that I actually felt the most calm. I responded to the challenge, as I had done all of my life. Almost no interview made me nervous—ironically, unless it was with a family member or someone I knew well. The most nervous I ever got on *Fox & Friends* was when my mom came on the show for a segment on preparing traditional Swedish Christmas foods.

Now that I was doing so many interviews on *Fox & Friends,* it really struck me in a profound way how important my violin training was. I learned how to do interviews in the same way I would perform a violin piece—by listening and being tuned in. I always prepared, but being in the moment was crucial because an interview subject might say something in the first sentence to throw you off. If you watch people doing interviews you can tell which people listen and which don't. Some cling to their set list of questions no matter what happens, which makes for a lousy interview.

Interviews can also run the gamut emotionally, just like different violin pieces. You might have a grandiose beginning, a melodic, emotional middle, and a fiery finale. I've learned to get into the rhythm.

When doing a particularly emotional interview with someone who has suffered a great loss or had a terrible crisis, I always say in some way at the beginning, "I can't imagine how you feel." Because I *can't*. The worst question that interviewers ask people in those circumstances is, "How are you doing?" Well, how the hell do they *think* they're doing? I never ask that question. I try to be in tune with the person—to get inside the moment and feel empathy.

When I get done with an interview, the most important thing the person I'm interviewing can tell me is, "Thank you so much for making me feel comfortable. I didn't even realize that we were on TV talking." It's similar to when I performed on the violin. I wanted to touch the heartstrings of the people listening so that they felt the emotion that I was feeling—to give them the same experience I was having on the stage.

The hardest interview I did while at *Fox & Friends* was with the mother of Christina-Taylor Green, the nine-year-old victim of the shooting in Tucson that wounded Congresswoman Gabby Giffords in 2011. The day after the shootings, Roxanna agreed to give her first interview to me. I was filled with nerves and dread. What were the right questions to ask a grieving mom who had just lost her beautiful child? What could I possibly say?

I was also fearful that I wouldn't be able to hold it together on the air. Kaia was eight at the time, and my sense of emotional connection was so great it was hard to breathe. As I was writing out questions for the interview during commercial breaks, I kept breaking into tears. I actually had to pinch my leg to try to stop myself from becoming too emotional. I said a prayer before Roxanna joined me on the phone.

In the interview I focused on who Christina-Taylor was and what she had accomplished in her short life.

"I just can't even put it into words," Roxanna said, in a heartbreakingly sad voice. "I can't express the devastation and hurt and how we were so robbed of our beautiful, beautiful princess. She was a beautiful girl, inside and out. She was so intelligent, and her light shines on all of us today and forever and I just have it in my heart that my angel is in the arms of my mom and my grandmother and our good friend Margaret up in heaven. I lost my mom a year ago, so I'm just trying to be positive and strong because that's what Christina-Taylor would want."

Roxanna and I talked about how her faith gave her courage. She told me that her daughter was going to do great things in heaven. "Maybe that's where she was needed. She's my angel."

A year later Roxanna returned to talk about the book she wrote about her daughter and the tragedy, called *As Good as She Imagined*. To prepare for my interview with her, I was reading the book at my kids' piano lessons, and I had to hide my tears. It is so painful to read but impossible to put down. There is one story that will stick with me forever. One month after Christina-Taylor died, Roxanna wrote that she received a message from her in a dream. She said Christina-Taylor told her that she was in heaven with her grandma and that she was okay.

Parents who lose a child, especially violently, are never "okay" again, but I respect and admire Roxanna Green for giving others who have lost a loved one a reason to keep going.

.　.　.

It was while doing *Fox & Friends* that I got a reputation for being a culture warrior. Bill O'Reilly started inviting me to come on *The O'Reilly Factor* for a regular culture warrior segment. I really cared about this stuff. Fox was the first place I'd worked where it was okay to talk openly about your faith on the air. Of course, I understand that when you're doing news reporting and anchoring, it's not appropriate. But at Fox I had a different kind of forum, so I went for it.

Where our culture is headed is an enduring topic of interest for many people, and I think they appreciate it that I take the topic on—even when they don't agree with me. For example, I've received plenty of flak for talking about the war on Christmas, often being described as "freaking out" and "going ballistic," as if I were some demented Christian warrior. One Web site published this pearl: "If Bill O'Reilly is the commander-in-chief of the War on Christmas, Gretchen Carlson is the head of the women's auxiliary." The thing is, it's not a joke to me. I can't think of a single other religion whose holy day is treated like a joke.

It all came to a head over the Festivus controversy. Festivus is a fake holiday, invented by the hit show *Seinfeld* in 1997. It was a funny bit on the comedy, and I laughed along with the rest of the world. But then it got real. Some people subsequently began to celebrate the holiday as an alternative to the Christian celebration, and one of them wrote a book called *Festivus: The Holiday for the Rest of Us.*

In 2008, when I heard that a group was petitioning the governor of Washington State to erect a Festivus pole as part of the Christmas display, I thought it was the stupidest thing I'd ever heard. When I brought it up on *Fox & Friends*, Steve and Brian tried to laugh it off as silly, but I was dead serious. I thought it was mocking Christianity, and I said so. (And by the way, a lot of people think that on Fox we have producers talking to us through our earpieces telling us what to say. We don't. That protest was all me.)

"I can't believe you guys are defending this," I said to my laughing colleagues. "I'm all for humor, and I'm all for telling jokes, but this is an insult to Christianity." I said I thought it was an outrage that my kids would have to grow up in a culture that forced them to grope their way past a Festivus pole to see a Nativity scene—on Christmas!

Festivus just wouldn't die. The worst episode came in 2013, when a group erected a Festivus pole that consisted of six feet of beer cans next to a religious display that included a Nativity scene, a menorah, and other religious symbols at the Florida state capitol. Again I spoke out, appealing very straightforwardly to American values and common sense. I was asking a question that needed to be asked: Do we think so little of our religious symbols and rituals that we would give equal weight to a beer can sculpture based on an old sitcom? I still think it's a good question.

I was gratified when the *American Spectator* published an article by Jeffrey Lord titled "Gretchen Carlson Is Right." Lord wrote, "Ms. Carlson's outrage was right on target. She is exactly right to look into the cameras and call for a stand-alone display of that crèche. She understands perfectly what it represents, and that without the reverence and respect of those values we are all in serious trouble." Amen!

My reputation as a culture warrior was one reason I got a role in the movie *Persecuted,* which was released in 2014. The film is a thriller that focuses on two rights in America that are sometimes taken for granted—freedom of religion and freedom of speech. The main character is an evangelist who is framed for a crime he didn't commit and persecuted for holding firm to his religious beliefs. In the movie I play Diana Lucas, a journalist who asks tough questions. It was fun doing the movie, but the topic also meant a lot to me. Every day in the news business, I report on stories just like this. Christians or people of other faiths are persecuted simply for standing up for something they believe. The intolerance seems crazy, but it's happening a lot more than you might think. The question *Persecuted* makes you ask is: Could the fictional movie plot ever happen here?

By the way, doing that movie was an example of how important it is to take on new challenges. I really stepped outside my comfort zone with *Persecuted*. Actors have often told me they had a hard time imagining doing live TV and ad-libbing on the fly. Well, I had the opposite struggle on the movie set. It was very hard to sit still for fifty takes.

After seven years on *Fox & Friends*, I got an incredible opportunity to host my own show. *The Real Story with Gretchen Carlson* premiered on September 30, 2013, at two o'clock in the afternoon. My kids were ecstatic because it meant I would be home in the mornings and could even drive them to school on some days. The simplest things in life have so much meaning. And Casey was very happy because I wasn't always stressed about being in bed by nine at night. I could be a regular adult.

On my first show I pointed to the "cozy chair" area on my set and asked my Twitter followers to send me their suggested names for the area. I was surprised and amused when one of the tweets came from Jon Stewart at *The Daily Show*. His suggestion: "Purgatory." I thought it was funny, and when I read some of the tweets at the end of my show, I included his, and with a teasing smile said, "I wonder if we'll add that to the mix." I knew he was kidding with his suggestion, and I was kidding with my response. But immediately my comment was picked up on the Internet, with one Web site displaying a banner headline: "Fox's Gretchen Carlson Confused by 'Daily Show' Punchline." Really? They didn't think I got the joke. This sort of thing is typical.

My new show has given me the opportunity to build on the strengths I learned on *Fox & Friends,* especially doing hard-hitting interviews, many of which have a strong emotional pull—such as conversations with veterans and an interview with parents who lost a child in the war. I've also created some interesting panels to really mix it up discussing current events. There's been a faith panel, a women's power panel, and a "manel," which is, you guessed it, a panel of men. I do a daily "My Take" at the end of the show, which is a commentary on one topic that I feel especially passionate about. Each day it's something different. One day it could be about politics, the next our education system—and some days I write about really personal messages, from my daughter's once being bullied to how important I think it is to stand up for Christian values. From the start I've wanted to showcase the *real* me, so I've included lots of personal segments, views behind the scenes, stories from home, and a blooper reel. I always share comments from viewers and am constantly looking for ways to make the show better. It's a work in progress and always will be.

The environment is very high energy. At our daily meetings people are expected to come in with ideas to pitch, and then we have to make sure we have all the elements—videotapes, rights, guests, and so on. This is TV, so the best idea in the world can die because the elements aren't there, or a guest we want books on another show. And, let me add, working in an environment where there's breaking news puts a whole new perspective on things. I could have the most amazing show planned and it can get scrapped in a heartbeat when an important world event occurs. It just goes with the territory. It's very challenging, but in my mind there is nothing as exhilarating as live TV.

When the weather got nice, I started going outside to the street to do segments like the one testing the fare of the food trucks (my favorite!). It takes a lot of machinations to get outside. One day I taped a video to show viewers just how hard it is. I had exactly three minutes to get from the set on the twelfth floor down the elevator to the street, change the microphone packs on the back of my bra, then race outside, get new mic packs, catch my breath, and start talking.

Having my own show has allowed me to lend my voice fully to the issues I care about. It's challenging to be on my own and to set my own style, but I love covering the important issues of the day in an authentic way.

Soon after I started my show, I made a big statement on October 11, which was the International Day of the Girl. I decided to go on air without makeup, to present a positive role model for young girls. It was a "first" on cable news! My guest on the show—also without makeup—was Jodi Norgaard, CEO of Dream Big Toy Company, which promotes self-esteem for girls. Norgaard told my viewers about the Brave Girls Alliance, formed to encourage the media and retailers to provide healthy messages and healthy images for girls. "Let's stop sexualizing our young girls, because it's not right," Norgaard said. I was proud to stand up as a role model in the fight to let girls be girls.

These days my mother has become an unexpected role model for me as an executive woman. Mom has always been amazing; she embraced her role in the home, and we were all better for her loving attention. But a few years ago when Dad decided to retire, Mom took over the helm.

Her motivation was in part inspired by the dramatic rescue of the dealership in 2009. That year, at the height of the financial crisis, General Motors announced it was terminating Main Motors' contract. That was crazy—the dealership had just hit 105 percent of its earning projection and was doing very well, even in the bad economy.

Some people wondered if my parents ended up on the hit list of dealerships shuttered because I worked at Fox News. I guess we'll never know, since there was no real formula for who got canceled and who didn't. I did an interview with my parents on *Fox & Friends* when they were in town one time after the cancellations had started. Their dealership had made it through the first two rounds at that point, but was terminated a few weeks after the interview. When they called to tell me they'd received the notice, I broke down crying. I just didn't understand how GM could close down a profitable business that had been in our family for almost a century.

My parents decided to fight. My mother proclaimed, "I will walk outside without any clothes on my back before I let this thing go under." Dad taped a moving appeal to Congress, and I even got in on the act, talking about it on air. Finally, thanks in large part to a phenomenal effort from the Minnesota congressional representatives, the contract was restored. In the process, my smart, outgoing mother became friends with every politician in the state and on Capitol Hill.

When they got the dealership back, my mother quipped, "I've never worked so hard to get back something I already owned." And with Dad in retirement mode she announced that she wanted to step in, at the age of seventy-three, and run the dealership. Mom has been hugely successful in that role, in large part because she understands people so well. Her philosophy is that running a dealership is about building relationships, both with the employees and the customers. She tells me that she loves going to work every day.

I have to smile sometimes, because Mom used to get so irritated when I was a young journalist talking about women's rights in the workplace. She'd say, "Gretchen, I wish you wouldn't talk so much about those issues." But now that she's running a company, it's a different story. She wants to talk about the ways women get treated differently in business. It's not just rhetoric to her—it's *real*.

When you ask viewers to invite you into their living rooms, you have to expect them to treat you with an intimacy that can be jarring. I love my viewers and fans, and their daily supportive messages really give me a lift. But in this era of social media, the flood of commentary that follows me through each day is not all love. Not surprisingly, many of the comments are not about what I say or the issues I discuss on the show, but how I look or what I'm wearing. No surprise—male anchors don't get the same scrutiny over their physical attributes. Aside from occasional comments about Brian's hair, I can't remember Steve or Brian receiving many comments about their looks in the seven years I sat beside them on the couch. But I sure did! Being on TV sometimes feels like a running fashion commentary:

"Gretchen needs a jacket . . . PLEASE!"

"Please sit up straight and look like a lady."

"You're a lovely woman, Gretchen. No need to expose yourself."

"You should NOT wear short skirts . . . ever . . . with your thunder thighs and legs."

"Just lose weight or cover up."

"Those are not arms for sleeveless styles."

Some of the comments veer away from the helpful and into the mean—not just about the way I look, but the content of my show and how I express my ideas. There's a tendency on social media to let the mockery get out of hand, and the fact that it's anonymous makes it easier for people to say things they wouldn't say to your face. My "Mean Tweets" segment on *The Real Story* is popular with viewers because they get it. One day when I tweeted I'd had a car accident on an icy road on my way to work, writing, "Nothing like seeing life flash before your eyes—thankful," one Twitter responder wrote, "Did you hit a Festivus pole?" Another person tweeted, "All about you, you did not have the accident, the driver did, your dumb blond life flashed? ha." On air I responded, "I've got news for you, that is not the first time I've heard a dumb blonde joke. Try somethin' else, somethin' new." It's important for me to occasionally air mean tweets. I can poke fun at myself and also expose social media bullying—to help young kids who face an ever-growing problem with this. I figure if I can be bullied relentlessly and feel the sting at my age, I can only imagine how it affects kids who are so vulnerable.

Truth is, it just doesn't bother me anymore. I think my mental attitude shifted when I turned forty. It doesn't matter so much what people say about me. I know who I am. But faced with the negative barrage of social media, I've also decided to inject a positive note. Most of these people don't expect to hear back from me, but when I get a particularly vicious comment, I'll respond to the person, "Thank you so much for writing. I hope you have a fantastic day." The strangest thing happens when I reply positively. Sometimes the negative commenters fall all over themselves to retract, writing, "Oh, I hope you have a good day too, I love your show and I was just pointing out that I thought maybe . . ." and then they are apologetic. It's cathartic to respond with a positive comment—and in an important way it helps break the cycle of meanness.

One of my role models in responding to mean comments is Carey Smith Steacy, a pilot for the Canadian carrier WestJet. After a flight, she was shown a note that had been scribbled on a napkin and left by "David," a passenger in seat 12E. He complained that WestJet should have told him there would be "a fair lady . . . at the helm" so he could have booked another flight. He wrote, "The cockpit of an airliner is *no* place for a woman. A woman being a mother is the most honor, not as 'captain.'"

Steacy's reply on Facebook was a brilliant example of a positive response: "To @David in 12E on my flight #463 from Calgary to Victoria today. It was my pleasure flying you safely to your destination . . . Funny, we all, us humans, have the same rights in this great free country of ours. Now, back to my most important role, being a mother."

The comment threads are not all snark, though—not even close. The best communications are the many wonderful letters and e-mails from my fans, who feel as if they know the real me. Sometimes it seems as if I am a part of their family. It always strikes me how little effort it takes to reach out to viewers in a personal way, yet how much it means to them. For example, I received a letter from a woman telling me that her elderly father was my biggest fan. The family was coming to New York to celebrate his eightieth birthday, and his only wish was to meet me. It was a no-brainer. I invited the family to the show and gave her father the star treatment, including presenting him with a birthday cake. Afterward, his daughter wrote me a beautiful, heartfelt letter about the visit: "Gretchen, I am sitting here writing with tears in my eyes as I am overcome with gratitude toward you. So many times I have wondered why someone like you would have done all of this for perfect strangers. You are truly an incredible person! Honestly, if we had won millions of dollars in a lottery it would not have matched the gift you gave our family in a single day."

Wow! Her letter made *me* cry. I don't have to wonder why I get up and do what I do every day.

CHAPTER 10

To Whom
Much Is Given

Catherine Violet Hubbard was a little six-year-old redhead with a bright spirit and a beautiful smile who loved animals. Grace Audrey McDonnell was a sweet-faced blonde, also six, with an artistic flair, who dreamed of being a painter. Both were gunned down on December 14, 2012, with eighteen of their classmates and six teachers in the Sandy Hook school shooting. As a family we shared the grief and outrage of the nation. As a journalist I struggled to keep my emotions in check while reporting the news. When my daughter decided to do something special as a tribute to Catherine and Grace, it was the proudest moment of my life.

Kaia is an extremely sensitive and caring young girl. Living in New York City when she was little, she noticed homeless people and asked me why they lived on the street. I tried to explain as best as I could, and she insisted on giving her own money to them when we passed by. Years later, after we moved to Connecticut, I was planning to meet Kaia and a friend and the friend's mother for lunch in the city after finishing up *Fox & Friends* for the day. They arrived fifteen minutes late. The other mom apologized with a smile. "Sorry we're late, but Kaia wanted to make sure we found enough homeless people to help with all the money in her wallet before we came to lunch." That's my daughter! She's always the first to reach out, whether it's giving money to the poor or packing up the clothes she's grown out of to take to the homeless shelter.

In the aftermath of Sandy Hook, Kaia, then ten, a serious piano student, had learned eleven classical pieces, and her teacher was urging her to do a solo recital. But she told me that she only wanted to do a recital if it would help somebody, and she came up with the idea of performing to raise money in honor of victims of Sandy Hook. Many of the children had charities formed in their memories, and Kaia studied their stories and chose Catherine's and Grace's charities because they touched her heart—an animal sanctuary in honor of Catherine and a playground and an art scholarship in honor of Grace. "I love animals and the arts," Kaia said simply, "and I wanted to give to charities that are things I like to do."

The recital took place at our church in May 2013, and Catherine's and Grace's families were in the audience as Kaia performed. We all had tears in our eyes, not only because the music was so beautiful, but because Kaia, a little girl herself, had orchestrated this remarkable event as a way of doing something to help.

In July 2014, Kaia and I visited the plot of land that will eventually be the Catherine Hubbard Animal Sanctuary in Newtown, Connecticut. It was a very moving day, and Kaia was thrilled when she was asked if she'd like to join Catherine's brother Freddy as one of the first two children advisory board members. I have a feeling that this work will be a part of Kaia's life for years to come.

I've carried the Carlson family dictum—"To whom much is given, much is expected"—with me as a core philosophy my whole life. When I think about it I can still hear the rich tones of my grandfather's voice as he preached about love and charity from the pulpit. I can see my parents opening their hearts and their checkbooks time and again to help others in our community in Anoka. I can recall the intense feelings of compassion when we traveled overseas and met families who could barely afford to put food on the table. We were blessed, and my parents were determined that we would not squander our good fortune or feel prideful, but learn humility and use our advantages to help others.

It is a lesson that Casey and I have passed on to our children. We have taken special care to see that Kaia and Christian are not swept up in the entitlement culture that is so prevalent today. Our life in the church gives us a way to practice daily charity. We are a family that volunteers—whether that's Thanksgiving dinner at our church or playing chess and participating in dance parties at homeless shelters. We teach our children that in giving back you are the winner too.

I learned that spirit of giving from my parents. Today they always tell me that my giving spirit is what makes them the most proud of me—not that I'm famous as a journalist on Fox News, or that I was Miss America, or that I was a concert violinist, but that I'm a good person. It's what I will someday say to my own children.

I believe that every person has something to contribute to the community and the larger world, which is why even with my full schedule I think it's important to do my part. It's why I'm on the March of Dimes board of trustees and also the board of directors for the Miss America Organization. When I moved to New York I started getting involved in the pageant again. During that time ABC was considering removing the talent portion from the broadcast, and a group of former Miss Americas got together and said, "Over our dead bodies." We managed to help put a stop to that idea and also lobbied for the organization to put a former Miss America on the board. I'm proud to say there are now four former Miss Americas on the board, including me.

For our family, faith is what binds us together. I always joke that some weeks I may not see Casey very much with our busy schedules, but I know I will almost always see him for our one hour at church on Sunday. Also, each spring we teach Sunday school together, switching off between our kids' classes. It's important for kids to see their parents at church. Studies show that when dad doesn't go to church, the kids end up not going either later in life. In our life together faith is the greatest gift we can give to our kids, realizing that there's a higher power and always something more important in your life than whatever you're going through each day.

I work on TV, but my most important job is being a mom. I think that's true of any woman with kids. We share a common purpose—to help our kids be the best they can be. But there is no clear road map, and it is up to each of us to find a way to instill core values in our children, and there is plenty of debate about how to do that.

A couple of years back I interviewed Amy Chua about her bestselling book *Battle Hymn of the Tiger Mother*. She wrote about being strict and demanding with her two girls. She did things like make them practice the violin and piano for three hours every day. Her parenting methods sent the nation into a passionate conversation about what it meant to be a good parent.

Most of the media was raking the tiger mom over the coals for her views on parenting. It seemed that all anyone could talk about was the fact that she didn't allow her girls to have sleepovers. I didn't necessarily agree with all her views, but when I interviewed Amy, I wanted to make sure she had a chance to tell the other side of the story.

Even one of my own colleagues disapproved. When I appeared on *The O'Reilly Factor* the night my interview aired, Bill didn't mince words. "Carlson" (he always calls me by my last name), he said, "you're a tough interviewer, but I think you were pretty easy on her this morning." I didn't really go easy on her, but I just wanted to be fair. I didn't like a lot of what she had to say, but I thought it was important to hear her out and try to understand. Maybe it was because I was also raised by a so-called tiger mother, only mine was a blonde, blue-eyed Swede.

Because of my music I had an unusual upbringing, with more responsibilities and pressures than my peers. Now that I'm able to look back on it, I see my childhood experiences as an incredible gift and wouldn't change them for anything. But when it came time to decide what I would carry forward into my own parenting, I had to make my own way, just like every other parent. In spite of my special circumstances, it feels as if my childhood in Anoka took place in a simpler time when values were closer to the surface and easier to express. Faith was a source of meaning, comfort, inclusiveness, and spirituality, not a political bargaining chip. I've heard people say that these are different times requiring new rules, but I wonder if that's true. There are new challenges, to be sure, but I view values as a stable force, not something to be swayed by politics, technology, or any modern contrivance. Rather than bend our values to fit the times, we need to fit the times to our values. When I ask myself what I need to do to be a good parent in any given circumstance, chances are I reach back to Anoka for guidance.

I know a lot of parents who want to be friends with their kids. As one told me, "We don't do consequences." I think she's fearful that her kids will stay mad at her. She wants them to think of her as a cool parent. I prefer the age-old wisdom by none other than Dear Abby: "If you want children to keep their feet on the ground, put some responsibility on their shoulders." The kids aren't always happy about it, but as I recently told my mother, "My kids don't like it at the time, but at the end of the day when I put them to bed at night, they still tell me they love me."

No question it's more difficult to be that kind of a parent. It's a lot easier to say "Okay" than "No." I thank my parents for saying "No" to me at times and providing me with a model of how to parent well.

It's the job of parents to teach children how to behave in the world, how to be kind and treat people with respect. If you don't teach them, they won't learn. I try not to let my kids get away with bad behavior. Recently, our family made a trip to Minnesota to visit my folks. I returned to New York early for work, and Casey brought the kids home. Later, my mom told me that after I left, Christian had been naughty one day when she took them out to lunch. I pulled Christian aside and said, "I heard about your behavior. Do you realize how lucky you are to have your grandparents in your life? They're my parents. Do you know how lucky I am to still have them in my life? Do you know how much they do for you in love? There's going to be a time that comes when they're not going to be here. You better be nice to them while they're here." Christian was tearful and ashamed by this point. I said, "You are going to call Grandma right now and you are going to apologize for your behavior."

Christian got on the phone, and he was very solemn and remorseful. "Grandma. Hi, it's me. I'm so sorry, Grandma. I didn't mean to treat you that way at lunch. I'll never do it again, Grandma." I hope he doesn't forget that lesson.

I believe that kids crave structure. They might fight it, but they do better with it. Actually, parenting experts have repeatedly said that this is true—that structure makes kids feel safe and allows them to build competence and confidence. That's one reason I have introduced music to my children at an early age. I'm not trying to force them into a role as concert pianists, but I believe studying music is a way to learn discipline in life. As I discovered, the skills learned practicing and perfecting a musical piece can later be used in how you do your job every day.

A few years ago, I found a great idea online for a sticker chart, which was a disciplinary tool, and I used it effectively for years. It was posted on the refrigerator, with a list for each child that included things like making their beds, practicing the piano, and not fighting. I could change the list with a dry erase marker, depending on the day. For each accomplishment I pasted on a sticker at the end of the day, and both kids watched my every move to see how many they would get. Four out of five stars earned them each a half hour of technology the next day. Less than four stars meant no Wii or iPad. Whenever they fell short, I'd hear a chorus of begging, but I held firm. It also gave me a way to control the use of technology, which has become one of the biggest issues parents face.

Personally, I have ambition for my kids to excel, but these days it's a challenge to define for them what excellence really means. My recent experience with Christian shows why. I took him to his hockey tournament at 5:45 in the morning, but I had to leave early to be with Kaia, so he came home with another family. When Christian walked in the door he had a medal, but he didn't seem as happy as he should have been winning the tournament. He said, "Mom, I don't get it. We won, but everybody got a medal, and they were all the same size, even for the kids who were on the fourth-place team. Everyone got the same medal and ribbon and you can't tell the difference between those who won and those who didn't."

I mumbled, "Welcome to 2014!"

I don't buy the idea that the way to build a child's self-esteem is to give him or her a trophy that isn't deserved. Having been a young competitor, I can't imagine how I would have felt had everyone in competitions been awarded the prize, whether or not they won. I know from experience how wonderful it is to compete and win, and while it is disappointing to lose, it's also an opportunity for parents to teach kids a very important lesson—that failure in life is a key to success.

When I teach this lesson to my children I tell them about an experience I had in the seventh grade when I ran for a student council position. My slogan was "Stretchin' for Gretchen," with a drawing of a person with an extra-long arm reaching up to put a vote in the ballot box. My dad helped me with the posters and the slogan. It wasn't easy finding a word to rhyme with "Gretchen."

When I lost the election, I was devastated. But my grandfather sat down with me that day and told me the story of Abraham Lincoln—about how many elections he lost before winning. I never forgot his advice and now I pass it on to my kids and use the example when I do motivational speeches.

It's come in handy. In the third grade Christian ran for treasurer of the lower school. His slogan was "Christian the magician. You can 'count' on me." He was so disappointed about losing that the next year he told me he wasn't planning to run for fourth-grade lower school president because he didn't want to risk losing again. So out came the Abraham Lincoln story, and he did run. He didn't win, but he gave it his all.

Losing is hard, but it's as important for kids to experience having to cope with failure as it is for them to win. When we praise mediocrity and give everyone a trophy, children don't learn how to deal with setbacks. They don't learn the meaning of taking risks. We rob them of the chance to participate fully in life.

When I was Miss America, I gave a speech to a huge Christian conference for teenagers. I spoke to them about failure, wanting to impress upon them the idea that you don't have to give up if you fail. It can be a learning experience that leads to success. I told them about being in the tenth grade and how all in one day I had three big failures: I didn't get the part in *Oklahoma!* I auditioned for a song and dance group called the Whirlwinds and I didn't get picked. I ran for homecoming attendant and lost. Failure upon failure. Then to top it off, the guy I was interested in called me fat. I could feel the audience responding. All kids know what it's like to not be picked, to be embarrassed, to get left out. I related my grandfather's Abraham Lincoln story. Then I turned it around and told them that it was those losses in tenth grade that spurred me to say, "I'm not going to be losing anymore." In the next two years I grew from the experience, and I got the lead in the play, I became a homecoming attendant, I won Miss T.E.E.N. Minnesota. I didn't let failure hold me back. Instead, it was pivotal to success.

Believe it or not, my favorite book as a kid was *The Little Engine That Could*. I actually use the story in my speeches now, because it ties in with my life story. That little engine didn't think he could get up the hill on his own, and the other engines didn't help him. They were mean and teased him. But it's all about perseverance and struggle and finally getting up that hill. That's the way I've lived—no matter what happens, I've kept pressing on, climbing that hill.

The truth is, even at this stage in my life I'm not immune to self-doubt. We all have those moments when we're afraid we're not measuring up or are worried that other people are judging us harshly. I still have bouts of insecurity when I have to give a speech or appear in public. Even when I'm the featured speaker, I feel butterflies walking into an event. Is it going to go well? Are they going to laugh at my jokes? Will they like me? The nerves never completely go away.

And I'm capable of having my feelings hurt. As a new trustee attending a dinner for my daughter's school, I heard that a woman in the room pointed to my name in the program book and said to her friend, "What do you think about *this*?" Her tone made her disapproval clear. It hurt me that because of where I worked or what I'd done in my life, I was automatically being judged as unworthy of being a good trustee, or, worse still, a positive role model for the girls at the school. Such judgments can feel cruel, and no matter who you are they sting. I imagined myself calling the woman and saying, "You don't know me. How do you know I won't be a good role model for your kids?"

I'm just like everyone else in that respect. I realize that there's a tendency for people to see public personalities as fair game for criticism and scorn, and our media culture feeds that. But I'm happiest when people see the real me and accept me for who I am outside the spotlight.

I have aspirations. I have future goals. Who knows what I'll do next? Maybe I'll find myself in the pulpit. Or in politics. Maybe I'll get that long-delayed law degree, or return to music. I do know one thing: I'll never stop growing. And I have a standard reply to people who downplay my efforts by saying, "It's easy for you. You're perfect." Well, guess what? Nobody's perfect, least of all me. I always joke that there are plenty of things I can't do. I can't parallel park. I can't drive a stick shift. I can't whistle. I'm lousy at doing makeup. I never learned to type correctly. And before I had two rounds of braces, I could fit my little finger between my two front teeth. But I embrace my imperfections, knowing I don't have to be perfect to follow my dreams.

Funny story. I also don't have fingerprints on my left hand. I found this out the hard way—by airport security. Casey and I were applying for security clearance at the TSA so we could go right through customs without all the rigmarole. Part of the process was getting fingerprints taken. Casey did his, then Kaia and Christian, and when the officer got to me there appeared to be a problem. She kept pressing my fingers down, over and over. "What's going on?" I asked. I had no idea.

She said, "Ma'am, I hate to tell you this. You have no discernible fingerprints." I stared at her agog. Kaia burst into tears. Did all those years of playing the violin shave off my fingerprints? I ended up getting a big X on my form, and Kaia was inconsolable. I tried to make a joke about it. "Hey," I told her, "I could have been robbing banks all this time."

Kaia howled, "Mommy, you want to be a criminal?!"

"No, I don't want to be a criminal," I assured her. The security agent was serious, but saw the humor of the situation. It all just goes to show that we really are unique as individuals. Just because I was missing that most common sign of uniqueness didn't mean I wasn't me. I've carved out my own path, shaved fingerprints and all.

I know one day—I'm sure before I'm ready for it—my children will carve out their own paths, just as I did. They will discover their callings. Ready or not, like it or not, this reality is as old as time. It is our job as parents to make sure they are equipped with a solid foundation that will hold them steady through the inevitable ups and downs they'll face.

And while my kids are making their way in life, I will be growing and changing too. I always want to be a person who seeks new challenges—who never feels too old to try something new. Or maybe even to rediscover something old.

The Music
of My Life

Alone in the house one Sunday, I was puttering around thinking about this book and my music. I was looking through some old musical scores, and on a whim I went over to the closet where I keep my violin and pulled it down. I hadn't taken it out in years, and now I carefully opened the case and got out my instrument. After such a long rest period, it was out of tune, so I spent some time tuning it. Then I went ahead and played a few notes from "Adoration," my old favorite. There was no problem remembering the notes, which were burned in my memory. But I knew it would take time to get my vibrato back. The vibrato is what sets you apart as a musician; it's your special quality, and I would have to practice steadily for months to restore it. Playing the violin is not like riding a bike. You can't pick it up years later with no effort and return to your previous level of accomplishment. And that was my great fear and frustration. I wanted to play like I used to. I wanted to feel the way I used to feel. Running my hands over the instrument, I felt that longing and the sadness of knowing I couldn't easily capture what I'd once had—if at all.

Writing this book brought up so many emotions. It made me realize how much the spirit of my music still lives in me. And as much as I love my work, nothing I've ever done in TV—even my biggest interviews on the world stage—has ever come close to moving me the way that some of those performances did.

I returned my violin to the case, and began going through a pile of CDs of my early performances. I grabbed a couple of them to play in the car that afternoon when I went to get a manicure. One was the Lalo performance with the Minnesota Orchestra when I was thirteen, and I put it in the player in my car. Probably not a great idea, because as I was driving through our little town, the tears were flowing while I listened to myself as a young girl playing my heart out. My sunglasses were fogged up, and when I reached my destination I sat in the parking lot listening to the end.

The entire time I was getting my nails done, my mind was a million miles away, remembering. I was eager to get back in the car and put in the next CD, which was my second performance before the Minnesota Orchestra when I was fifteen. For the life of me I couldn't remember that performance or why I was playing for the orchestra again, but the quality of the tape was much better and I could hear how much I had matured in my playing since the first time. I think by then I had moved to a full-size violin, and I could hear the depth of the notes and the improvement in my vibrato.

That night we were going out to dinner as a family, and I decided to leave the CD in the car player for my kids. They'd never heard me play before. Casey, Kaia, and I got in the car; we were picking up Christian from a birthday party before heading to the restaurant. When I turned on the player, Kaia asked, "Mommy, what's that music?"

Filled with emotion, I replied, "I just want you to hear this. This is Mommy playing with the Minnesota Orchestra when I was fifteen years old."

"Oh," said Kaia noncommittally.

Then Christian got in the car, and he asked, "What's that music?"

"That's Mommy playing."

"It is?"

"Yes. You want to listen to it?"

"Uh, okay."

Then the kids began chattering in the backseat, and Casey turned to me and started a conversation about the next day's schedule, and I realized that I was the only one listening to the music. My wonderful husband and my beautiful children just didn't get it. I was transported back to the emotions I felt as a child—that feeling of being alone with my gift that nobody else understood.

Briefly, I felt sorry for myself, but then a light broke through. I had an epiphany. The music that poured from that CD was music that forever played within me. It wasn't necessary for my husband or my children to listen, or to appreciate it at that moment. I knew it was there. I knew what the music represented and what it had meant to me. The young violinist I once was informed the adult that I had become, and it was all good.

Rarely does a day go by that I don't visualize myself playing out my original dream. I'm standing on the Carnegie Hall stage as one of the greatest violinists in the world. That didn't end up being my real life, and I don't regret it. But all those years dedicating myself to the violin shaped who I am. Someday I just may pick up the violin again and bring my story full circle, dust off the strings for good and let the music sing. But for now I am content, and immensely grateful for everything I have, including the gift of being the real me.

ACKNOWLEDGMENTS

At every time of my life I have been able to follow my dreams and achieve my goals because people believed in me. My parents raised me with values, love, and a religious foundation. They also taught me the importance of giving back and making the most of my God-given talents. Mom, thank you for instilling in me the drive and perseverance to push ahead no matter what, and for telling me I could be anything I wanted to be. You are my best friend and confidante, and I love you more than you will ever know. (Thank you, as well, for having the dedication to create the twenty scrapbooks of my life that helped so much in putting together this book!) Dad, you are an amazing man. I have always been so proud to call you my father. I adore you more than you will ever know—for your humility, your humor, and your huge heart. I have truly been blessed.

Because of the loving support of my parents and grandparents, I had the confidence to study the violin at age six. It never occurred to me that I couldn't do it. Thanks to the tremendous guidance and training from Ken Davenport, Jeanette Simmons, Mary West, Thelma Johnson, Dorothy DeLay, Lea Foli, Cliff Brunzell, Dr.

Henry Charles Smith, Dr. William Jones, and others, I was given the gift of music that has stayed with me all of my life. A special thank-you to my friend and world-class pianist Randall Atcheson for also teaching my children the miracle of music.

Being Miss America was an important achievement—and I couldn't have done it without the violin. I am grateful to the organization for inspiring young women to be the best they can be and am proud to serve on the board of directors. In particular, I want to thank Sam Haskell; Sharon Pearce; Leonard Horn; members of the board; the first Miss America, Margaret Gorman (1921) for being just five foot one; the entire Miss America sisterhood; Miss America volunteers everywhere; my travel companions, the late Ellie Ross and the late Anita Puhala; Mike Tracy; Kathleen Munson; Stephen Yearick; my Miss America hostesses, Carol Adams and the late Marge Howell; my Miss Minnesota host family, Faye and Lowell Anderson; my Miss Cottage Grove pageant directors, the late Sue Bargsten and Ron Bargsten; my fellow Minnesota Miss Americas, Dorothy Benham and BeBe Shopp; and the wonderful volunteers for Miss Cottage Grove and Miss Minnesota. I'd also like to thank the Brandes family for introducing me to the Miss T.E.E.N. program, showing me I could use my violin talent to achieve a new kind of goal.

In my career as a television journalist I owe a lot to the mentors who have reached out to me and the colleagues who have helped me and made my work better along the way: at WRIC-TV in Richmond, WCPO-TV in Cincinnati, WOIO-TV in Cleveland, KXAS-TV in Dallas, CBS News in New York, and of course Fox News. In particular, I want to express my gratitude to Jody Lomenzo, for pointing me in the direction of a career in television news, and to my former bosses, all of whom inspired me in their own unique ways: Wayne Lynch, Joyce Reed, Jim Zarchin, Greg Caputo, Kim

Godwin-Webb, Joe Duke, Bill Mondora, Steve Friedman, Michael Bass, Pat Shevlin, Marcy McGinnis, and Andrew Heyward. A big thank-you to all of my former co-anchors, producers, and camerapersons, especially cameraman Steve Stewart in Dallas, my CBS *Saturday Early Show* co-anchor Russ Mitchell, and CBS producer Carrie Rabin Aber.

Special thanks to Fox News CEO and chairman of the board Roger Ailes for continuing to believe in me and giving me the opportunity to do what I love every day; Executive Vice President of Programming Bill Shine; Vice President of Programming Suzanne Scott; Executive Vice President of News Michael Clemente; Vice President of News Jay Wallace; Executive Vice President Legal and Business Affairs Dianne Brandi; the entire *Fox & Friends* crew and producers, as well as hosts Steve Doocy and Brian Kilmeade; *The Real Story with Gretchen Carlson* crew and producers, including Executive Producer Jennifer Williams and Producer Kenneth Tucker; Bill O'Reilly for giving me the platform to be a culture warrior; Greta Van Susteren for inspiring me with her incredibly hard-work ethic; Bill Hemmer for twenty-five years of friendship; and everyone else at Fox—on and off the air. Thanks as well to the fantastic Fox News hair and makeup teams past and present, including Maureen Walsh, Jeisohn Fiala, Anita Torres, Erica Colon, and Daniela Zivkovic. Thanks to my amazing assistant, Linda Haviv, and to my agent, Sharon Chang, for her years of guidance and support. I also remain thankful to the women who have inspired me in television news, especially Diane Sawyer, Kathie Lee Gifford, Deborah Norville, and Barbara Walters.

I couldn't do what I do without the support of my wonderful friends—specifically my sister, Kris Carlson-Germain, and Molly Kinney-Leonhardt—as well as my many friendships, which span the country, especially my friends in Greenwich, Connecticut, and

New York City. Thank you to the community of Anoka, Minnesota, and to all of the people at Zion Lutheran Church in Anoka and First Presbyterian Church of Greenwich. I am also grateful to my teachers, especially Jack Nabedrick, for giving me my motto in life: *Carpe diem!* A special thanks to Dr. Francine Blei, the hemangioma doctor who helped bring my family through a very difficult period. And to my wonderful nanny, Tara Santos, for dedicating the last seven years to taking such great care of my kids.

Like every other area of my life, I've found that writing a book involves the efforts of many people. I am deeply grateful for all those who believed in me and my message: my brilliant and caring literary agent Bob Barnett, the devoted Viking publisher Clare Ferraro, and my wonderful and insightful editor, Carolyn Carlson. I am also appreciative of others who made this process work, especially Catherine Whitney, who spent countless hours helping me get it all together, sharing her wisdom and writing expertise, and most importantly becoming a great and trusted friend.

Finally, I am thankful every day for Casey, Kaia, and Christian, who fill my days with the only things that really matter—love, laughter, and meaning.